The Concise Guide to Teaching Composition

Derek Soles
Drexel University

PEARSON
Prentice
Hall

Upper Saddle River, New Jersey 07458

© 2007 by PEARSON EDUCATION, INC.
Upper Saddle River, New Jersey 07458

ISBN 0-13-233755-X

Printed in the United States of America

CONTENTS

PREFACE

About two-and-a-half million students take first-year composition each year in America, and some 45,000 professors, graduate students, adjuncts, and nontenure-track faculty teach them. They do outstanding work, but they are often distracted. Graduate students are struggling to finish their own degrees, write their dissertations, and, in many cases, raise a young family. Adjunct, nontenure-track faculty are underpaid, so they often must work at more than one institution to make ends meet. Many of them are recent graduates striving to find a tenure-track position at a college or university. Some are MFAs, trying to establish themselves as writers, sacrificing writing time to the time-devouring demands of teaching written composition. Many tenured professors who teach first-year writing are experts more in literature than in composition.

These literature professors, graduate students, and adjunct faculty who teach college composition in this country have little time to study composition theory, read the professional journals, attend workshops, and reflect upon pedagogy, but they do want to teach their classes competently and professionally. For them, I have written this book. *The Concise Guide to Teaching Composition* is a brief, straightforward introduction to composition theory, and, especially, pedagogy. Its purpose is to help harried writing teachers teach their classes effectively, by providing them with some basic theory in written discourse and some useful information and advice about various teaching strategies that work effectively in the first-year composition classroom.

I have taught first-year composition for nearly thirty years. I have taught undergraduate and graduate courses in composition theory and practice for almost as long, and I have served as First-year Writing Director at a large state and a large private university. Here, in essence, is my advice, my seventeen guidelines for teaching college composition:

1. Understand the nature of the writing process.
2. Establish clear, relevant goals for your students to realize.
3. Provide students with a comprehensive course syllabus.
4. Use textbooks that are right for and that appeal to your students.
5. Vary your teaching methods so you reach *all* of the students in your class.
6. Assign as much reading as the course can accommodate.
7. Assign topics in keeping with the goals of your program.
8. Teach students how to reflect upon and research a topic.
9. Teach students what plagiarism is and why it is wrong.
10. Insist students revise (not just edit) their writing.
11. Provide *practical* instruction in the conventions of Standard English.
12. Encourage students to give each other constructive feedback on work in progress.
13. Help students cultivate a writing style that animates their work.
14. Share with your students the criteria you use to evaluate written work.

15. Grade student writing in a way that supports instruction.
16. Understand the benefits and drawbacks of using technology to teach writing.
17. Learn the discourse conventions in a variety of academic disciplines.

I devote one chapter in *The Concise Guide to College Composition* to each of these guidelines.

Chapter One
THE NATURE OF THE WRITING PROCESS

Composition teachers must have a basic understanding of the nature of the writing process. This knowledge will help you plan your curriculum, implement effective teaching strategies, and evaluate your students' work. Writing is a complex process, consisting of three overlapping and interrelated competencies: it is one-part craft, one-part cognitive exercise, and one-part social transaction.

Current-Traditional Rhetoric

Before the dramatic increase in composition theory and research which has occurred over the last forty years, English educators viewed writing as more craft than art, an almost mechanical, bottom-up process of crafting words into sentences, sentences into paragraphs, and paragraphs into essays, letters, reports, and the various other longer forms of written discourse. To be effective, a writer needs to know the conventions of language: how to use and spell words correctly; to form complete sentences, free from errors in grammar, structure, and punctuation; to write unified, coherent, and well-developed paragraphs. This approach is usually known as **current-traditional** theory, an oxymoronic label perhaps, but one that indicates that the theory has historical validity, has the authority of tradition behind it, but is still relevant today, still "current." Indeed, the best selling composition handbooks, still staples in most writing courses, still assume an essentially current-traditional pedagogy.

Current-traditionalism is seriously limited but is neither wrong nor, as some advocates of other theories contend, counterproductive. Students do have to learn the conventions of sentence and paragraph construction. Spelling counts, as do proper grammar, sound sentence structure, cohesive paragraphs, correct punctuation. Instruction in the qualities of correct writing—of Standard English—should always be a part of a writing curriculum. There is some controversy over the hegemony of Standard English because it is sometimes viewed as the code that the privileged race and class adopted and now impose upon those with less social, economic, and political power. While the charge may be true, it is unlikely to change the fact that business, government, and schools and colleges conduct their business in Standard English and that, to achieve social and economic status and success, students need to learn the Standard English the current-traditional approach privileges.

One problem with current-traditional theory is that it implicitly endorses the notion that writing is a linear step-by-step, sequential process, that, in other words, a writer first reflects upon his or her topic, then does some research, then makes a plan, then writes a draft, then revises the draft, then edits the revised draft and, finally, publishes his or her finished product. But research indicates that writing is not a linear, but a **recursive process**.

The pioneering research of compositionists like Janet Emig, Sondra Perl, and Linda Flower radically altered our view of the nature of the writing process. In the 1960s and 1970s, researchers studied writers at work, interviewed them, had them talk about the processes they were invoking as they were working on a written text. This research revealed that writing is much more of a recursive than a linear process. Writers do not first generate ideas, then find a thesis, then plan, then draft, then revise and, finally, edit. Writers revise and edit while they draft. They discover ideas while they draft. They often alter, even discover, their thesis as they draft. They might make a preliminary outline, but other components of the composing process often inspire useful changes to the outline and force the writer to return to and alter the original. While working on a body paragraph, a writer might get an idea for a more effective opening and abandon the body paragraph to revise the opening before going back to the body paragraph. A writer might be in what she believes to be the final stages of the writing process when she finds a new source that forces revision to what he or she has already written.

This insight was revolutionary and helped to prompt the infamous "paradigm shift" in composition theory and pedagogy. Most English teachers work from the premise now that writing is not a step-by-step, linear, sequential process but a recursive process, a form of organized chaos, more like running a maze than a marathon.

Of course, the syllabus for a writing course should not be a maze. It needs to have order and structure, usually established by subdividing the components of the process into pre-writing, writing, and revising strategies. But remind your students often that, even though there are recognizable <u>components</u> to the writing process, there are not stages to the writing process. A pre-writing strategy such as planning is ongoing; a plan can change during the writing "stage." Similarly, revision can occur and does occur while a writer is drafting. Students are actually pleased to learn that writing is a recursive process. It's liberating. They have to have a plan but the plan can evolve while they write; they have to revise but they can do so while they draft. Freed from the notion that writing is a rigid, sequential process, student are, as Mike Rose has shown, less likely to be apprehensive about writing and less likely to suffer from writer's block.

Another problem with current-traditional theory is that it diminishes the complexity of the writing process. By stressing mechanical correctness, current-traditional theory undermines the cognitive dimension of the writing process and downplays the role the reader has in influencing and shaping a text.

A Cognitive Process

As writing teachers we know, intuitively, that writing is a mind game, an often intense **cognitive process**. Linda Flower and John Hayes have done the best job of mapping the cognitive processes writers invoke as they work on a text. After studying carefully the ways in which writers actually work, they attempted to construct a model of the writing process. Their model is initially intimidating, identifying as it does twenty components to the writing process, divided, subdivided, and interconnected in intricate ways. But the writing process is complex and anyone who attempts to model it is bound to create a complex matrix. And, despite its complexity, the Flower and Hayes model is decodable, and it does help writing teachers appreciate the nature of the task they are asking their students to undertake.

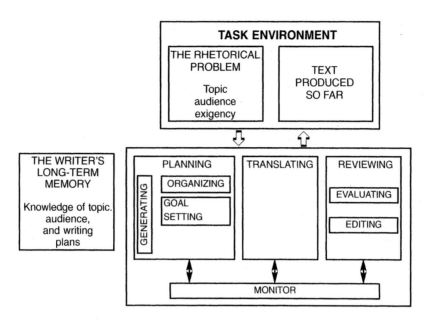

Figure 1 A cognitive process theory of writing (Flower and Hayes, 1981)

The largest box in the Flower and Hayes model explains the immediate writing process. It is subdivided into four additional boxes. One box represents planning, one drafting (their term is "translating"), and one reviewing. Within the planning box are boxes for organizing, goal setting, and generating; within the reviewing box are additional boxes, one for evaluating and one for revising. So far, then, their model is standard current-traditional theory. But the fourth main box within the writing process rectangle represents the monitor, and here Flower and Hayes bring real insight into the process. The monitor guides the writer as she juggles the three main processes of planning, drafting, and reviewing, helping her decide when she must invoke which component of the process to create a competent text. The monitor confirms the recursive nature of the writing process, discussed above. The monitor also suggests the metacognitive dimension of the writing process.

The second large rectangle in the Flower and Hayes model represents the task environment, the context within which writing takes place. Context includes the rhetorical problem, subdivided into topic, audience, and exigency, which is the motivation writers must summon to get words onto paper. This rectangle also includes the evolving draft of the written discourse the writer is producing, that is the "text produced so far" (256). The Flower and Hayes model has been criticized for undervaluing the role social context plays in the writing process, but when the model first appeared, in 1981, its recognition of the task environment within which a writer works was somewhat ahead of its time.

The third major component—the third big rectangle—in the model represents the writer's long-term memory, which is subdivided into knowledge of topic, audience, and writing plans. Knowledge of writing plans means that the writer understands that written discourse needs structure and knows there are alternative structures—temporal or hierarchical, for example—within which he or she can shape his or her text. Two-way directional arrows connect the long-term memory box to the writing processes box, which is, in turn, connected with two-way arrows to the task

3

environment box. Again, the model insists upon the interconnectivity of the components of the writing process.

The Flower and Hayes model gives us an understanding of the many components of the writing process and helps us begin to understand the complex ways in which these components act and interact. The model asks us to consider including instruction in our writing courses on how to use the writer's monitor most effectively, perhaps by modeling the writing process for our students as we compose a text on the blackboard or overhead, while we simultaneously talk about what we are doing, explain why we are making the decisions we are making, and indicate why we are invoking this component of the writing process at this time. The model insists we include context in writing instruction and that we help students activate their long-term memories to help them find the ideas they need to write well. The model underscores the extent to which writing is a cognitive process, that developing students' cognitive capacity is an important function of teachers of writing.

A Social Transaction

Cognitivist theory privileges the writer, suggesting as it does the solitary author deep in thought puzzling out an intellectual or personal issue or problem. In the 1980s, some compositionists began to critique cognitivists on the grounds that they focus too much on the mind that creates a written text and not enough on the society that shapes the mind. Writing, these theorists argue, is more a social than a cognitive process or, at least, is first a social and second a cognitive process. They came to be known as social-constructivists because the essence of their theory, their motto, is that knowledge is socially constructed. Knowledge is created within a social context and sanctioned by the social group to which the learners belong. This knowledge consists not only of information but also of ways of expressing that information to others. A good writer gives the social group for whom he or she is writing knowledge and information the group needs and expects and expresses that knowledge and information in a way sanctioned by the group. Members of a college/university community, for example, write articles, lectures, and reports in Standard English, expect their members to do the same, and reprove them if they do not.

Kenneth Bruffee; James Berlin, who calls it "social-epistemic" theory; Patricia Bizzell; and David Bartholomae are among the leading exponents of social contructivism as it applies to written composition. They are critical of the cognitivists and their notion of thought as a personal construct and an individual vision of reality. They argue, instead, that thought is "an intellectual artifact constructed by social interaction within a particular community of discourse" (Connors and Glenn 147).

Consistent with their belief that learning is a social process, social constructionists advocate a collaborative pedagogy. One manifestation of a collaborative pedagogy is the peer response group, which consists of three or four students who read and constructively critique the drafts of each other's written work. Peer response groups help students learn and understand why their written work is or is not communicating effectively to others in the discourse community and how to make changes to their writing so that it will meet the needs and expectations of readers. In other words, peer response groups urge a sense of audience onto student writers, and students do write more effectively when they have a strong and clear sense of audience. Some writing teachers question the benefits of peer response which is often little more than the awkward sharing of perfunctory praise. And, indeed, there is some research, which questions the efficacy of peer response, but there is, as well, a considerable body of research in support of peer response (see Spear; Trimbur; Howard, all of whom advocate peer response but discuss its drawbacks, as well). Distilled, this research suggests that peer response is an effective instructional strategy when teachers provide explicit instruction for students on how to respond intelligently and insightfully to the work of their peers, limit peer response sessions to two or three aspects of good writing, and monitor carefully the dynamics of the groups to keep them focused, on task, and on track (see Chapter Twelve for a full discussion of peer response).

Another manifestation of a collaborative pedagogy is the collaborative writing assignment. The collaborative writing assignment can be anything from an in-class paragraph a group composes, an essay, which a small group writes together and receives a common grade for, to a complex research project that requires students to delegate responsibility to each other to complete the various parts of a writing project. In *Singular Texts/Plural Authors*, Lunsford and Ede note that collaborative writing assignments help prepare students for professional careers, since managers often assign a task to a team of employees who must work together to complete a project which, more often than not, contains a written component. Their book includes a list of interesting collaborative writing assignments.

Post-Process Theory

In recent years, this focus on writing as a social transaction has been responsible, in part, for the emergence of a new theory of writing, known as the post-process movement. Like the social constructionists, post-process theorists believe that writing is a public, social activity, though they move beyond the social constructionists in the extent to which they also believe writing is interpretive and situated (Breuch 110). Writing is public because composing a text results more from our interactions with others than from our own consciousness. It is interpretive on the part of both the writer who re-interprets the social and written texts he or she is familiar with and the reader who re-interprets the new text not in light of any knowledge of any stable external truth but in light of his or her ever-changing experience with other social and written texts. It is situated in that it is mediated always by the immediate context or situation—both personal and social—within which the act of writing occurs. Because the act of writing is so indeterminate and amorphous, dependent as it is upon social influence, subjective interpretation, and ever different contexts, many post-process scholars believe that teaching a writing "process" is a futile activity.

Lee-Ann Breuch disagrees, arguing instead that post-process theory "encourages us to reexamine our definition of writing as an activity rather than a body of knowledge, our methods of teaching writing as indeterminate activities rather than exercises of mastery, and our communicative interactions with students as dialogic rather than monologic" (98-99). Indeed, her pedagogy makes lemonade out of the sour lemons post-process theorists have grown. Writing may be an indeterminate activity that cannot be mastered, but that does not mean a post-process pedagogy cannot be developed; it simply means pedagogy must evolve to take into account post-process insights. Post-process theory urges us to

reconsider teaching as an act of mentoring rather than a job in which we deliver content. To think of teaching as mentoring means spending time and energy on our interactions with students—listening to them, discussing ideas with them, letting them make mistakes, and pointing them in the right direction. (120)

Her preferred pedagogy, then, is one-on-one, and consequently he or she champions writing centers which " provide a concrete context for post-process theory because one-to-one interactions are the primary practice of writing center tutors" (120). Initially, Breuch's argument hardly seems radical since most universities support writing centers. But his or her argument suggests that universities make the writing center the true center of writing instruction, fund it generously, staff it with highly qualified tutors, and relocate it from the basement, where it is too often found, to the penthouse.

Post-process theory does add an interesting new dimension to our understanding of the nature of the writing process. It builds upon and expands social epistemic theory. It challenges the work of the cognitivists and the current-traditionalists, though the former have the authority of social science behind them, and the latter can still point to the best selling handbooks as evidence of their continuing influence. The best we can do, amidst these theory wars, is to consider and reflect upon all theories that attempt to explain the purpose and the process of written discourse and shape our curriculum accordingly. Writing is a craft and, as such, has rules for assembly writers need to know. Writing is a multi-dimensional cognitive process and writers need to know how to juggle the many components of the process to write successfully. Writing is a social transaction and writers need to know how to connect with and influence their discourse community. Consider all theories as you plan your course and you will design one that is based upon but ultimately greater than the sum of its theoretical parts.

Chapter Two
THE GOALS OF A FIRST-YEAR WRITING PROGRAM

The goals of first-year writing programs around the country are diverse and ambitious and are influenced by the values and the political disposition of the policymakers. Conservative first-year writing program administrators want their faculty to teach students how to write effective academic discourse, so students will do well throughout their college years. Often, they hope, as well, that the writing skills students acquire in their composition classes will translate to the business community and will help their students become successful professionals. Expressivist program administrators want their faculty to help students use writing to uncover personal identity, acquire self-knowledge, puzzle out their place in the world. More radical first-year writing program administrators want their faculty to make students aware of the systemic social injustice—the racism, sexism, classism, and homophobia—that pervades contemporary American society and to develop Marxist and/or feminist-inspired courses that will help students challenge and resist the established order, which is too white, heterosexual, and patriarchal. Practical, progressive-minded program administrators often add an outreach service-learning component to their program, whereby students go into the community beyond the college to assess and assist with the literacy needs, usually of those who have not had the benefit of a college education.

Write an Effective Academic Essay

In a first-year writing program, students should be taught the components of the process of writing academic discourse, especially the academic essay requiring research. Most program administrators want instruction in the conventions of academic discourse to be one goal, if not the primary goal, of the first-year writing sequence. If this is a goal of your program, you will be responsible for teaching your students how to:

- generate ideas by reflecting upon topic, audience, and purpose and by using such heuristics as freewriting, webbing, and questioning (specific instructional strategies will be offered in Chapter 8);
- acquire authoritative and reliable information from libraries and the Internet and cite this information, using a citation method developed and sanctioned by a professional organization such as the Modern Language Association or the American Psychological Association (specific instructional strategies will be offered in Chapter 8);
- draft effective introductory, body, and concluding paragraphs (specific instructional strategies will be offered in Chapter 10);
- revise their work (specific instructional strategies will be offered in Chapter 10);
- edit their work (specific instructional strategies will be offered in Chapter 11).

The sequential nature of this list is misleading, in that it implies that writing is a linear process. But, as the evidence discussed in the preceding chapter indicates, writing is a recursive process. If you want to, or if you are required to provide instruction to your students on the components of the writing process in an orderly manner, using, for example, the top-down structure presented above, remind your students regularly that, while good writers will invoke each component of the process, they will do so chaotically.

I prefer to provide, in the course of one class period, some instruction and practice in more than one component of the writing process and to vary methodology among lecture, small-group work, and whole-class discussion (discussed in more detail in Chapter 5). This method reinforces the recursive nature of the writing process and, given the variety of knowledge shared and activities partaken, makes the class more interesting and enjoyable.

Write Well at Work

Some English educators argue that, by teaching students the components of the process of writing an academic essay, we are preparing them, as well, for the professional writing they will be required to do when they finish college. Others insist discourse is context-specific, that every field has its own discourse conventions, instruction in which we cannot hope to include in an already full first-year curriculum. The truth lies somewhere in between. Students should be able to apply some of the knowledge they acquire in their first-year composition classes to some business, technical, and professional writing circumstances, and they should be able to adapt some of what they learned in first-year composition to complete other job-related writing assignments.

Specific, direct instruction in the various genres of business, professional, and technical writing is rare in first-year programs, and when it is present it is usually restricted to the business letter, especially the letter of application. Most of the handbooks the major publishers offer to first-year writing programs provide at least one chapter on business writing. The extent to which composition teachers assign these chapters varies widely from program to program.

Foster Personal Growth

In some first-year writing programs the main goal is to show students how their writing can empower them. Composition teachers who adhere to this philosophy are usually called "expressivists." Writing, the expressivists believe, is an extension of self, of a self trying to come to terms with its place in the world, trying to foster and understand its values, attitudes, and ideals. We write to puzzle out the world, to understand it and our place within it. Expressive discourse privileges the writer, "using language to assert the self" (Lindemann 58).

D. Gordon Rohman was an early advocate of this theory, writing in 1965 that we must teach writing to enlighten students about "the powers of creative discovery within them. . . . What we must do is place the principle of actualizing in the minds of students and the methods of imitating it in their hands (in Young 37). Donald Steward echoes Rohman, arguing that "the primary goal of any writing course is self-discovery for the student and that the most visible indication of that self-discovery is the appearance, in the student's writing, of an authentic voice" (in Young 38). Gere traces expressivism to the work of John Dewey who "emphasized the learner's experience, interest, and motivation and encouraged teaching that centered on the student rather than on the discipline" (20). Its influence grew in the wake of a conference of English educators held at Dartmouth in 1966. The conference was organized in part as a reaction to a call from English teachers who felt the current-traditional model was not meeting all of their needs. American and British educators attended the conference, and the Americans learned from their British counterparts that there was another approach to the teaching of writing, a student-centered approach, which encouraged students to use writing as a way of discovering and dealing with their personal issues and concerns.

Expressivism has its critics who argue that it is the nature of writing teachers to romanticize their craft, and that their aphorisms about writing and personal voyages of discovery are somewhat supercilious. Expressivist theory, they argue, is more suitable to realizing the goals of a creative writing class than to a first-year composition class, where a key goal is to help students do well by teaching them some conventions of academic discourse. But there is no doubt that expressivist theory continues to influence the composition curriculum. Indeed, Richard Fulkerson argues that "expressivism, despite numerous poundings by the cannons of postmodernism and resulting eulogies, is, in fact, quietly expanding its region of command" ("Composition at the Turn of the Twenty-First Century" 655). Its influence continues to be seen especially in the focus on the personal narrative essay and in journal writing. Narratives and journals are at the center of the expressivist curriculum, though many teachers who would not necessarily think of themselves as champions of the expressivist movement have appropriated them, reconstituted them in light of their own teaching philosophy, and integrated them into their own curricula.

Promote Social Justice

Some English educators believe that, because a writer joins a discourse community when he or she composes and publishes a text, he or she acquires the ability and the right, even the responsibility, to participate in transforming that community (Lindemann 34). An influential group of these "social constructionists" believe that this ability to transform community through written discourse is the primary function of writing and the primary goal of a writing course. And they are very specific about the nature of this transformation. They share the belief that American society is systemically racist, classist, sexist, and homophobic, and that writing teachers are perfectly positioned to reform social injustice. They are known as radical or confrontational or critical teachers, and they consider themselves part of the critical cultural studies movement in composition studies (Fulkerson, "Composition at the Turn of the Twenty-First Century" 659). They put the proactive chicken before the reactive egg, arguing that since language shapes society, language can be used to reform society. Through its discourse, a society can choose, as it usually does, to reproduce its dominant ideology or it can choose to disrupt its dominant ideology. Radical teachers agitate for the latter and design their curricula to help foster such disruption. For them, the purpose of a writing course is to radicalize students—to shake them out of their middle-class complacency, make them see the social injustice that pervades their world, and urge them to reform society by exploring, in writing, the causes and consequences of its undemocratic foundations and by suggesting solutions to social problems. There are essentially two related schools of radical pedagogy, one feminist, the other, Marxist.

Feminist teachers believe that writing programs, influenced by their social context, have traditionally privileged a masculine pedagogy and writing style, characterized by a strong, authoritative voice, and a rigid structure. A feminist pedagogy and writing style, characterized by a cooperative as opposed to a competitive classroom ambience and a narrative, emotional, and digressive voice has been undervalued.

Collaboration is a hallmark of a feminist pedagogy, privileging as it does cooperation over competition. Peer conferencing is hardly a radical instructional activity; it is endorsed and practiced by many English teachers who would not necessarily label themselves feminist. But its ubiquity in the contemporary writing classroom is partially a result of recent feminist influences in curriculum design. Feminist scholars and educators have also been instrumental in advocating the elimination of the exclusive use of the masculine pronoun as the sole referent for a gender-neutral noun. If language shapes society, as the social constructionists argue, then a society that regularly refers to a doctor or manager or soldier or CEO as a "he" or a "him" is shaping and reinforcing a sexist and patriarchal world. Feminist pedagogues also tend to downplay argumentative writing, claiming that the virtues of a strong argument—a strong sense of authority, a detached logic, and a robust structure—are stereotypically masculine and so validate the virtues of an inherently repressive patriarchal society. They prefer to have their students write personal narratives and to keep journals where feelings and emotions are validated. They assign readings by women about women's struggle for equality and typically assign topics related to the women's struggle for equality and democracy.

Marxist pedagogues support feminist goals, but they paint with an even broader radical brush, including race and social class in their indictment of modern American society and in the list of issues that need to be addressed and reconsidered in the composition classroom. Marxists believe that the academy reflects and perpetuates systemic social injustice, and that it is the job of the writing teacher to alert his or her students to the existence of this social injustice, and to work with his or her students to reform their communities. They teach writing as a form of social protest, convinced that the student writer's first responsibility is to enlightened social change. They view knowledge as a socially constructed commodity, produced by a ruling class that sanctions and validates racism, sexism, classism, and homophobia through the discourse it produces. The student writer's task is to challenge this knowledge and to re-create it so that freedom and democracy may prevail in all aspects of society.

Marxist pedagogy is difficult to describe because any form of predetermined and proscribed instruction is antithetical to Marxist ideals. Indeed, a Marxist compositionist would likely argue that once a curriculum is established, it is, by definition, oppressive and in need of reform. Berlin describes a typical curriculum as "always open-ended, receptive to the unexpected, and subversive of the planned" (697). But there are some basic Marxist pedagogical principles to which such teachers adhere. Marxists believe in the sharing of power, for example, so they usually give students a say in the design of the curriculum, the design of policies to govern such things as attendance and late papers, the number of assignments to be completed, the manner in which those assignments will be graded, and the choice of readings. Given this inch, of course, students might be inclined to take the proverbial mile, a possibility radical teachers counter by acknowledging some need for control but by moderating the anti-Marxist implications by calling it "emancipatory authority." While validating choice, Marxist teachers do usually insist upon essay topics related to solving the world's problems—especially those caused by corporate capitalism—and usually assign readings that apply left-wing ideology to contemporary issues.

10

Radical pedagogy is, not surprisingly, controversial. With varying degrees of emotion—from outrage to mild disdain—conservative compositionists question the premises from which their radical colleagues work. Have the vast power of corporate capitalism and the military-industrial complex really forged a culture that is systemically unjust and undemocratic? Is the average American college student really oppressed? And are not those who truly are oppressed, by virtue of their race or class, in college to become a part of, not to overthrow the corporate capitalist establishment? Others object to the indoctrination that accompanies a Marxist pedagogy, and note that Marxists would be the first ones to object if a teacher used his or her classroom to advance a conservative Christian or a pro-choice agenda. Others wince at the self-serving connotations of phrases like "emancipatory authority" and "liberatory pedagogy," which makes Marxist teachers sound like the white knights of the Academy, rescuing oppressed, enslaved, and brainwashed students from a backward culture.

Fulkerson suggests that this critical cultural studies movement reflects "content envy on the part of writing teachers" ("Composition at the Turn of the Twenty-First Century" 663). College teachers are intellectuals who would rather teach and talk about great ideas with their students than teach them the prosaic components of the writing process. But the result, Fulkerson continues, is "a 'writing' course in which writing is required and evaluated, but not taught" (665). He has a second concern: CCS programs may be replacing liberal education with indoctrination:

> Teachers dedicated to exposing the social injustice of racism, classism, homophobia, misogyny, or capitalism cannot perforce accept student viewpoints that deny such views or fail to register their contemporary relevance. (665)

CCS teachers swear they are open to opposing point of view from their more conservative students. But "a socially committed teacher will rarely find contrary views presented by an undergraduate to be sufficiently 'thoughtful' . . . [and] a student who knows his or her instructor's own political views will probably not choose to oppose them with a grade at stake" (666).

Lad Tobin suggests a link between a critical cultural studies curriculum and the post-process movement, discussed in Chapter One. It is the post-process champions, he argues, who insist first-year writing courses must have more intellectual content and who have decided that content will be political. Like Fulkerson, he is critical, proclaiming that "organizing a course around a huge collection of readings that are chosen and controlled by the teacher and that reflect the teacher's interests and agendas sets back composition pedagogy thirty years—no matter how hip or leftist or progressive the readings are meant to be" (14).

While its critics do make a case, a CCS approach to the teaching of writing does have a place in a writing curriculum. A university is a stereotypically liberal space, and radical solutions to social problems often appeal to young people. Marxist/feminist teachers validate the views of many students who finally get the chance to explore in writing their own attitudes to popular culture and their own solutions to social ills. They also rile up others but, in the process, engage students in the content of the course, in a way more conservative teachers do not. A student who challenges his or her teacher's views is thinking critically and is motivated to write, if only to convince his or her teacher that there are better solutions to social problems and some redeeming social value in popular culture. And with their emphasis on cooperation and collaboration, radical teachers are in the vanguard of social constructionist pedagogy.

11

Serve the Community

Service learning or outreach, whereby students go into the community beyond their colleges and offer assistance to individuals and organizations, who need the kind of help students in a writing class are in a position to offer, is becoming an increasingly common aspect of advanced writing courses. But some first-year programs are also requiring students to do some community service work as part of the requirements for completing the first-year writing sequence. The work usually involves helping individuals and organizations with various literacy needs: writing letters, fliers, pamphlets, speeches, newspaper articles; reading aloud to the blind or the elderly; tutoring children and recent immigrants in reading and writing.

Such programs help fulfill several goals of a first-year writing program. Students who are helping others learn to write are reinforcing classroom lessons in a dynamic setting. Those who are ghostwriting letters and articles are applying, in a practical way, the knowledge they acquired in the writing classroom and further developing, among other abilities, a clear and strong sense of audience. Nearly all outreach programs require students to keep a detailed journal recording their experiences and reflecting upon their significance, and service learning experience provides a rich source for journal content. Some programs require a research paper, part of which requires some analysis and synthesis of their experiences as outreach literacy activists.

Outreach programs have their critics who argue that it may be presumptuous to assume that college students can help poor unfortunates who live beyond the ivory tower; less educated does not necessarily mean less literate. Some who teach in single-semester first-year writing programs argue that they barely have enough time to teach essential writing skills, that to send students to work off campus cuts too much into regular classroom time. Conservative compositionists connect service learning to critical pedagogy and see in outreach programs an ulterior motive, the dissemination of a radical political agenda. Even some radical teachers have expressed concern that students are not learning the lessons their community service is supposed to be teaching them, that, for example, they tend to blame the individual for illiteracy and not the society that is so complicit in fostering social injustice.

But to proponents of service learning the benefits far outweigh these drawbacks. Thomas Deans argues that community-based composition courses reveal the value of experiential learning and break down barriers between the academy and its surrounding communities. Outreach programs validate, as well, the role writing and rhetoric can play in solving community problems and in promoting social justice in general. Cooper and Julier, similarly, have students in their Public Life in America course write research papers that focus on community issues, requiring students not only to seek conventional sources in the library and online but also to conduct interviews and surveys and attend public meetings to gather the material they need. Students at once learn how to write an academic essay and how to participate as a responsible citizen in a democracy.

Corollary Goals

In the process of achieving the specific goals, described above, of a writing program, teachers will help students achieve three essential corollary goals: how to **read actively**, **think critically**, and use **technology** discriminately.

Most of the goals discussed above presuppose the need for active reading. To write a good academic essay, a sound business letter, an insightful personal narrative, students need to study good examples of each genre, to read them in a way that facilitates imprinting. Active reading includes teacher-led discussion of the general nature of a text prior to reading; dynamic activities such as note taking, underlining, and annotating while reading; and responding to questions and engaging in discussion after reading. By including such pre-reading, reading, and post-reading activities in the first-year curriculum you will make it easier for your students to emulate the exemplary texts they are studying. Chapter Six discusses in more detail the reading-writing connection, in the context of a first-year writing program.

Critical thinking is another important corollary goal of a sound first-year writing program. For an academic writing assignment, students often have to develop and sustain an effective argument. They therefore need to learn the basic principles of reason and logic, and they need to know how to recognize and avoid logical fallacies. A fun and effective way to help students cultivate critical thinking skills is to organize debates on current social and political issues. To be effective in developing critical thinking skills, debaters must research their topics thoroughly, and debates should be planned and structured to include a clear resolution and time for cross-examination and rebuttal. All students should participate in teams of three or four, and, when they are not debating, should play the role of audience members who cast votes at the conclusion of the debate to select the winner. Mercadante champions debating as an effective way of developing skills in critical thinking, analyzing and synthesizing knowledge, and extemporaneous speaking, and he recommends college teachers follow the rules and procedures of the Cross Examination Debate Association to maximize the learning opportunities debates offer.

The final corollary goal of an effective first-year writing program is to help students achieve a certain level of computer literacy. I say a certain level because some first-year programs now include instruction in website design, PowerPoint presentation, and other relatively sophisticated computer applications. Certainly students should acquire such relevant and practical knowledge, but there are limits to the first-year writing curriculum, even in a year-long program. Students should learn how to use the Internet to conduct research and must know how to tell an authoritative and reliable online source from an unreliable one. They should know how to access and use their textbook's website, and they should know how their or another university's online writing lab (OWL) can be used to answer their composition-related questions and help them as they draft and revise their work.

Clearly, contemporary composition theory offers writing program administrators quite a menu of goals from which to choose as they design and develop their programs. Indeed, the "WPA Outcomes Statement for First-Year Composition" is rapidly becoming obsolete, in that it has little to say about technology, social justice, and personal growth and nothing to say about community service. There are two schools of thought about the variety on the writing program goals menu. One school argues that we are losing our way and becoming too diffuse, that effective writing, not politics or technology or community service, must remain the focus of a writing program. The other argues that variety is good, that schools have the opportunity now to develop unique programs in keeping with the unique interests of their students and the mission of their college.

Chapter Three
DESIGNING THE COURSE SYLLABUS

The syllabus for a first-year writing course is usually between four and twelve pages in length and provides students with essential information about the content of the course, the assignments students must complete, and the policies and procedures the professor expects students to follow. A carefully designed and comprehensive syllabus will contribute to your success as a teacher. Your students will enjoy your course more, and you will enhance their chances of completing your course successfully if they know from day one what the goals of the course are, what projects and assignments they have to write and when they are due, what exams they have to write and when they will write them, what books and articles they have to read, what policies they will have to abide by.

The Content of a Good Syllabus

As part of their study on syllabus content, Becker and Calhoon reviewed syllabus literature and developed a list of twenty-nine items most likely to appear on a college-course syllabus (3). They then asked 863 students taking an introductory psychology course at one of four colleges or universities to rate the importance of each item on the list. Students used a seven-point scale, a 7 representing a great deal of attention, a 1, no attention at all. In descending order of importance, as rated by students, here is the list of the 29 items:

Examination or quiz dates
Due dates of assignments
Reading material covered by each exam or quiz
Grading procedures and policies
Type of exam and quizzes (e.g., multiple choice, essay)
Dates and times of special events that must be attended outside of class
Number of examinations and quizzes
Kind of assignments (e.g., readings, papers, presentations, projects)
Class participation requirements
Amount of work (e.g., amount of readings, length and number of other assignments)
Whether extra credit can be earned
Makeup policy
Late assignment policy
Attendance policy
Schedule of topics to be covered
Course format (e.g., lecture, discussion, videos, classroom activities)
Where to obtain materials for the class (e.g., texts, readings, lab materials)

Days, hours, and location of class meetings
Pre-requisite skills and course work
Course goals and objectives
Holidays
Course description
Instructor information (i.e., name, title, office location, phone number, e-mail address)
Available support services (e.g., tutoring, computerized study guides)
Instructor's office hours
Academic dishonesty policy
Course information (course number and title, section number, credit hours)
Drop (withdrawal dates)
Titles and authors of textbooks and readings (6–7)

The mean rating for the first item on the list—examination or quiz dates—was 6.67; for the last—titles and authors of readings—3.52.

We must, of course, be circumspect in applying the results of Becker and Calhoon's study to the design of a syllabus for a writing course. Our initial impulse may be to make certain we include all of the items on the list they have compiled and to sequence them on our syllabus in the order of importance, as determined by the students' ratings. But three of the top five items on the Becker/Calhoon list relate to exams and quizzes, which most writing teachers do not give as often as do colleagues in other departments. Moreover, basic principles of document design dictate that we begin a syllabus with the title of the course and information about the instructor, even though students gave low-importance ratings to these items. But if we adapt Becker and Calhoon's work to our own needs as writing teachers, we should produce a syllabus, the template for which, would look something like this.

My University

Department of English

Course Syllabus

ENGLISH 100: First-Year Composition

Professor:

Office Number:

Phone:

Email:

Office Hours:

IMPORTANT DATES

REQUIRED TEXTS

GOALS OF THE COURSE

CLASS SCHEDULE

Present material to be covered for each week or each class. (I prefer a syllabus organized weekly, because this allows for some flexibility in the way I can allocate time.) Include topics of mini-lessons, homework assignments, time devoted to peer conferencing, journal prompt, reading assignments, writing assignments.

Note if a major assignment is due, even though the date will also be included in list of important dates, above.

Indicate if there is anything special about this week or this date: last day to withdraw without academic penalty, no class due to holiday, etc.

General Guidelines for Essay Assignments

Include information about acceptable methods for citing sources, proper format, whether you expect hard copy or will accept emailed assignments. Remind students of late paper policy and plagiarism policy.

Criteria for Grading Essays

Include rubrics that will be used to assess each major assignment.

Plagiarism Policy

Late Paper Policy

Attendance Policy

The University Writing Center

Include information about location, hours of operation, website, how to make an appointment to see a tutor.

Final Grade Evaluation

Include each assignment and number of points and/or percentage of final grade each assignment is worth.

The professor reserves the right to include, in the course, information not included in this syllabus and to omit information that is included.

Your Syllabus as a Legal Document

Note that our syllabus template ends with a disclaimer, indicating that the professor reserves the right to make changes to the course content, while the course is taking place. Although, as Faye Hardy-Lucas notes, "a syllabus is not considered to be a legal document, it is a good safe practice, in a litigious society, for you as a professor to treat it as one" (1). She goes on explain that, in cases of educational malpractice, the courts have been reluctant to view a course syllabus as a legal document because:

1. There is no satisfactory standard of care by which to measure an educator's conduct.
2. Permitting such claims would flood the courts with litigation and would thus place a substantial burden on educational institutions.
3. The courts are not equipped to oversee the day-to-day operation of educational institutions. (1)

She also notes, however, that a Faculty Handbook is considered to be a legal document and that it is essential that professors follow any guidelines for syllabus design presented therein. She recommends, as well, that if you do have to change your syllabus during the course, the change should be to the benefit not the detriment of your students (2). And she cautions that, although courts have so far been reluctant to see the syllabus as a legal document, there may be a trend to find universities liable in tuition refund cases. She offers several "preventative strategies" to forestall the possibility of legal action:

❏ . . . provide the requisite number of hours of instruction for your course and cover certain course topics in classroom lectures, especially those topics which have been promised in course offerings found in the college catalog, course syllabus, or . . . on your . . . Web page.
❏ Insert disclaimers in your course syllabus regarding your right to modify the class schedule when necessary and your freedom to cover course topics as you wish.
❏ Communicate with your students. Remember the obligation of fair dealing. If changes are made to your syllabus, make them for student fairness only. (3)

The Tone of Your Syllabus

To help your students get the most out of your course and to anticipate and impede complaints that might otherwise arise, your syllabus must be thorough and accurate. But this does not mean its tone has to be harsh and severe. Surf the Web, access university websites, browse some of the faculty syllabi on the site, and you will find numerous examples of syllabi that sound as if they were written by a drill sergeant. "Attendance in this class is compulsory. . . . If you violate the attendance policy, you are subject to the following sanctions: . . . ;" "You will submit, on the times and dates specified on the assignment sheets, three essays . . . students who fail to submit essays on the times and dates specified will be punished. . . ;" "Regular and thoughtful participation is required . . ." Words like "compulsory," "sanctions," "failure," "required," "punished," conjure up the image of the schoolmarm, on guard in front of the class, pointer in hand, ready to smack any child who steps out of line.

Your syllabus is your first emissary, and you want it to convey the impression that you are a firm but positive and supportive teacher. Until they prove you wrong, you will assume your students will be attentive, will participate, will be responsible about attending class and submitting assignments on time. Here, for example, is the schoolmarm's attendance policy:

> Attendance in this class is required. If you miss more than 20 percent of class time, due to excused OR unexcused absences, you will be penalized one full letter grade. If you miss more than 30 percent of class time, due to excused OR unexcused absences, you will be penalized two full letter grades.

Here is the policy of the firm but positive and supportive teacher:

> Please attend class regularly. You will get more out of English 100 and you will not miss handouts and other important information if you make the effort to attend. In this class, students who attend regularly get higher grades than those who do not. If you do miss more than 20 percent of class time, due to excused or unexcused absences, you will be penalized one full letter grade. If you miss more than 30 percent of class time, due to excused or unexcused absences, you will be penalized two full letter grades. If you miss too many classes due to serious extenuating circumstances, please have your academic advisor contact me.

The second example does not simply boss; it justifies the policy, indicates rewards for following it, and provides some hope for students who might have experienced a personal crisis.

A sound syllabus is worth the time and effort it takes to compose. You can set a positive tone for your class, anticipate and curtail complaints about course content, and provide your students with a course table of contents if you design a clear and thorough syllabus.

Chapter Four
SELECTING EFFECTIVE TEXTBOOKS

Most first-year writing programs require students to purchase a handbook, a reader, and a rhetoric. Handbooks generally provide instruction and exercises in the use of Standard English, and so focus on teaching students how to recognize and avoid errors in grammar, sentence structure, paragraph structure, mechanics, and punctuation. The readers usually offer a variety of classic and contemporary essays, which serve as models for students to emulate and as sources for ideas and information they can incorporate into their own assignments; some readers include a selection of short stories, some even include poems and plays. Rhetorics focus on instruction in the components of the writing process, typically providing information on generating ideas for a writing assignment, conducting research, structuring a written text, finding a thesis, drafting, revising, editing, and citing sources. Many rhetorics focus exclusively on one rhetorical mode, the most common being the persuasive—the word "argument" appears in the title of many rhetorics. Rhetorics and handbooks are often combined as a single text. There are even some texts that combine all three of the genres.

There are, by my estimation, currently on the market some 2,000 textbooks designed for use in first-year composition programs. The journal of the Writing Program Administrators, *Writing Program Administration*, publishes a useful annual annotated bibliography of writing textbooks, but the authors do not include all currently available titles. There are hundreds each of the handbooks, rhetorics, readers, and combination texts currently competing for the attention of those first-year writing teachers, who are responsible for selecting texts for America's two-and-a-half million first-year writing students. Some schools have committees that select common texts for the whole first-year writing program; others allow each instructor free choice in text selection. Odds are you will be in a position, either as a committee member or an instructor at a free choice school, to select textbooks for your first-year writing classes. One purpose of this chapter is to provide you with some guidelines that will help you sift through the dozens of examination copies your publishers' reps will send you and select the best texts for your writing courses. Another is to suggest ways textbooks can be used to enliven and enhance instruction.

The Goals of the Program and the Needs of the Students

If there were a formula for text selection in a first-year composition program, it would triangulate the literacy levels of the students with the goals of the program and the cost, length, readability, and content of the texts available. Consider, for example, the textbook needs of a large urban community college that has a disproportionate number of minority, ESL, low-income, first-generation college students and that has a two-semester first-year writing program, the first semester focusing on narrative and nonresearched writing, the second on the academic research paper. Compare this to the needs of an Ivy League university, many of whose students are affluent, dominant-race overachievers, attending a university whose first-year writing program eschews narrative writing and has, instead, a two-semester program that focuses first on expository academic then on persuasive academic writing. Somewhere in between is the good state college, populated by a fairly diverse mix of middle-class students, completing their first-year writing requirement by taking a one-semester course that is a general introduction to academic writing. Clearly, these programs would require different textbooks.

For that first-semester course on narrative and nonresearched writing, for example, program directors at the urban community college would likely look for a reasonably priced, well-organized (possibly tabbed) combination handbook/rhetoric, written in a style accessible to minority students. For that first-semester course on expository academic writing, program directors at the Ivy League university would worry less about cost and acknowledge the profile of their typical student by searching for sophisticated and challenging texts. Finally, for the single-semester academic writing course, program administrators might combine a comprehensive rhetoric/handbook with a comprehensive reader.

Clearly there are differences among the thousands of first-year writing programs in the country and enough variety in the selection of available textbooks that the needs of virtually any program can be met. Composition textbooks are criticized because they often seem to be descended from if not cloned from some master text written years ago (Miles 32), and, hence, seem interchangeable. It is true that basic content is similar, especially from one handbook and rhetoric to the next. It is also true that a stable essay canon for first-year composition has gradually evolved (Bloom 407) and that many readers include many of the same canonical readings. But the different handbooks and rhetorics do tend to stress different components of the writing process and different readers privilege different themes. The texts differ, too, in style and readability, with some texts aimed at a basic college reader and others written for students at a more sophisticated reading level. You have a lot of choices. The key, again, is to find books that are appropriate for your school's demographic and your program's goals.

Additional Guidelines for Selecting the Right Textbooks

While program goals and student demographics are the essential considerations when you are selecting textbooks, there are other important issues you might want to consider as you are making your decisions.

Writing teachers are naturally tempted by texts that are written in a style and that contain readings that appeal to them. This makes good sense because if the teacher is enthusiastic about the content of a text, he or she will communicate this enthusiasm to his or her students, and thereby make it easier to engage them. It is important, however, to try to put yourself in the position of your students and select handbooks and readers with content that will appeal to first-year college students, content they can relate to. The best texts are those that manage to meet the goals of the program while engaging the interests of the teacher, but, especially, of the students

As a general rule, avoid a text that contains more than a thousand pages, unless it is a good combination text. Remember there is only so much content you can cover in a twenty-eight or thirty week academic year, and, for freshman, at least, it is better to cover the basics thoroughly than all of the particulars superficially. Humongous texts are usually expensive hardbacks. And it's disheartening to look out your office window and see a group of eighteen-year-olds trudging slowly across campus, their backpacks weighed down by three or four of these massive hardbacks. Students should not be overloaded with texts.

When you are reviewing a text for possible adoption, carefully examine the book's apparatus, its end-of-chapter exercises, its website, its instructor's manual. You want exercises that engage your students while they reinforce the instruction you have provided. You want a website that provides relevant and useful supplementary information and, especially, one that is easily accessible, that does not require a complex series of commands to access. You want an instructor's manual that provides a variety of classroom-tested pedagogical strategies you can adapt to make your own classes better.

Work with your book reps. I am always surprised to hear book reps tell me stories about the supercilious attitude they get from many professors who are clearly annoyed when salespeople interrupt their busy schedules. In my experience, the reps know their products well and will work with you to find those texts that are right for your program. They will happily send you examination copies of well-established and new texts that complement the goals of your program and the needs of your students. And, when you write your own book, they can be your first line of offense, performing the invaluable service of making certain your manuscript gets into the right hands, a service they will be more willing to undertake if you have established a good rapport with them.

Using Textbooks to Support Instruction

If you have selected textbooks that meet the criteria discussed here, you have invaluable teaching tools at your and your students' disposal. The handbook is the reference book of the first-year writing class. You may not use it much in class to provide direct instruction, but you will refer students to it as they work through end-of-chapter exercises, and you will reference it frequently in the marginal and terminal comments you make on their writing assignments: "Sarah, these are subordinate clauses, not complete sentences. Please review carefully Chapter 17 of our handbook."

The rhetoric is the manual of the first-year writing class. It supplements your instruction on the components of the process of completing successfully writing assignments in various genres from the narrative to the expository to the persuasive. You will likely assign chapters from the rhetoric for homework reading, and then generate whole-class discussion about the content of those chapters. In my experience it is not a great idea to read to your students directly from the rhetoric, more than a paragraph or two during class or to ask them to read aloud from it to the rest of the class. As important as it is, the content is not usually engaging enough, when read aloud, to hold student attention for too long.

The reader is the book that appeals most to students, containing as it usually does, interesting pieces on current social issues, popular culture, and personal, human-interest experiences. It usually provides models of good writing for students to try to emulate and information they can use to bolster the content of an assignment in progress. In class, then, you want to generate whole-class and/or small-group discussion, using your own prompts and those provided by the question that usually follow the readings, to focus on both the content of the readings and the rhetorical strategies the writers use to render the content readable. Readers are more engaging than rhetorics, so it may be good to read passages from the articles aloud and to call on students to do the same. There is circumstantial evidence, at least, that suggests that some students learn to revise their writing more effectively when they have practice and experience reading aloud (Moran).

Handbooks, rhetorics, and readers do not, in and of themselves, teach students how to write well. Students learn how to write through active engagement in the recursive processes of thinking, reading, planning, drafting, revising, and editing, in tandem with the support of peers and teachers who, at regular intervals, offer feedback on the developing text to help the writer make certain him or her work is fulfilling him or her purpose in a style that facilitates him or her readers' understanding. What good textbooks can do is provide supplementary instruction to your students as they learn to marshal effectively the components of the writing process and provide support for you as you guide them along.

Chapter Five
ACCOMMODATING STUDENT LEARNING STYLES

As a writing teacher, you have an array of methods and techniques for interacting with your students. You can interact with a whole class, encourage students to interact with each other in small groups, tutor students individually. You can lecture, ask questions, generate discussion, facilitate group work, stage a debate, show a movie, organize a field trip. You can speak to your students in the voice of a drill sergeant, a cheerleader, a coach, a mentor, a guide. Many writing teachers have a favorite way to configure a class, a favorite method of imparting knowledge, a preferred voice in which to speak, but I recommend you speak in many voices, at different times, in different ways, to all of your students together, some of your students in groups, and each of your students as individuals. There is so much diversity among students in a writing classroom—especially a first-year writing classroom—that a writing teacher needs to take an eclectic approach and use a variety of teaching strategies, if he or she is to connect with all of his or her students.

Not everyone agrees. Some writing teachers think that lecturing is a waste of valuable time that could be spent actually planning, drafting, and revising a text, perhaps with input from peers and the teacher. Hillocks reviewed the research on four methods of teaching writing and concludes that the "presentational mode . . . dominated by lecture and teacher-led discussion about the characteristics of good writing" (194) is the least effective method. More effective are the natural process and the individualized modes. The natural process mode is "characterized by freewriting about whatever interests the students, feedback from peer groups and the teacher, and opportunities to revise or redraft in light of peer or instructor comment" (194). The individualized mode uses teacher-student conference as the primary method of instruction (194). But the most effective method of teaching writing, according to Hillocks, is the environmental mode, which uses group work but in a more structured way than the natural process teachers do, specifically "to engage students with each other in *specifiable* processes important to some *particular aspect* of writing" (122) (italics mine). Other compositionists echo Hillocks' findings, referencing studies that suggest that the retention rate for knowledge acquired from a lecture is weak (MacLeish in Foster 209). And we have all attended lectures at conferences wherein the lecturer discusses the ineffectuality of the lecture method.

Similarly, some writing teachers cast doubt on the efficacy of collaborative learning and writing. To be sure, the educational zeitgeist is that knowledge is socially constructed and consequently there are more supporters than detractors of peer conferencing, collaborative learning, and collaborative writing. But even those who write in support of peer conferencing acknowledge its pitfalls (see Spear; Trimbur; Howard). Some students are reticent about sharing their work with their classmates; some students distrust the opinions of their classmates and prefer the authority of a teacher's feedback; peer group discussion too often begins with perfunctory praise about each other's work, then drifts into talk about who should be the next American Idol. Done right, advocates insist, the collaborative method is a most effective way of helping students learn to write. But it works better for some students than for others.

The one-on-one conference method, one teacher working with one student as he or she drafts and revises his or her paper, would seem an ideal way of improving writing skills, and certainly this method has enthusiastic advocates (Foster 198). An instructor using this method typically meets with each of his or her students each week for fifteen or so minutes, the amount of time usually dictated by the number of students for whom the teacher is responsible. Usually the tutorial is spent discussing a paper the student is currently working on, the teacher asking questions and offering advice. Such individual attention helps convince students their teacher cares about their development as a writer and might help motivate students to do good work. This method also allows the teacher to intervene while the student is drafting and revising, so it validates the process approach to writing instruction. On the other hand, the interpersonal dynamics of this method can be counterproductive because the student and the teachers are not meeting as equals. The teacher is the expert reader/evaluator to whom the student brings his or her work. There is a danger that the teacher might exert too much control and usurp the student writer's voice (Foster 201). But some teachers are so convinced of the efficacy of this method that they are willing to sacrifice hours of class time to meet with each student individually. And most colleges have a writing center where a student can go and meet with a tutor and receive more feedback on a work in progress from an expert reader.

But no one method of teaching writing works well for all students; composition teachers need to have a big bag of pedagogical tricks. We know—from the work of learning style experts—that different students have different learning styles. Writing teachers need to adopt an eclectic approach to teaching writing to accommodate the variety of learning styles students bring with them into the classroom.

Anthony Gregorc

The work of Anthony Gregorc, for example, illustrates the extent to which different learners perceive and organize knowledge in different ways. Some students see knowledge as concrete and tangible; others perceive knowledge as less tangible, more abstract. Some students feel compelled to organize knowledge sequentially if they are to learn effectively; others can learn while still preferring and appreciating the nonlinear, random, unclassifiable nature of knowledge. In Gregorc's taxonomy, there are four different learning styles: Concrete Sequential, Concrete Random, Abstract Sequential, and Abstract Random.

Concrete Sequential learners like teachers who lecture a lot because they learn best when an authority figure presents clear and specific information to them in a structured manner. They are passive but still efficient learners. A lecture can engage Concrete Randoms and Abstract Sequentials to an extent, the former because they appreciate tangible knowledge, the latter because they appreciate order and structure. But these are active learners who crave more variety. A lecture does not engage Abstract Random learners. They are bored by and unresponsive to specific information presented to them in a well-structured manner by one person, needing instead the stimulation of others in a more informal context.

Concrete Sequential learners do not like group work. Devoted time managers, they find peer conferencing inefficient and prefer to have their work reviewed by their teachers not their classmates. Concrete Randoms generally enjoy and benefit from group work because they need readers to suggest to them accepted ways of structuring their written work more effectively. As participants, they are great at suggesting to classmates alternate but still effective ways of structuring a writing assignment. Abstract Sequential learners generally do not benefit from group work because they tend to be naturally good writers, adept at transforming the abstract into the sequential, usually the very purpose of an academic writing assignment. But other group members benefit from the participation of Abstract Sequentials who are good at assessing the strengths and weaknesses of their peers' writing. Abstract Random learners enjoy group work the most, probably because they benefit the most from it. Their attention span lengthens when they are interacting with peers so they can heed the advice they are given more effectively than they can when listening to a lecture. They are also the best participants not only because they are so creative and perceptive, but also because they are sensitive and can convey suggestions and advice in a nonjudgmental, nonthreatening manner.

Concrete Sequential learners appreciate a one-on-one session with their teacher because it gives them the opportunity to clarify the nature of the assignment and to make sure they are efficiently meeting the needs and expectations of the person who will be evaluating their work. They are less eager to spend time with a tutor in the writing center. One-on-one instruction—with their teacher or with a writing-center tutor—is good for Concrete Randoms, who often need help shaping their ideas in a conventional way. Abstract Sequential learners are independent by nature and keen and able learners, and they rarely seek out individual help, unless they must. Abstract Randoms need one-on-one instruction the most. They enjoy personal attention and need it to focus and relate their ideas to their thesis and to present the ideas in a logical, coherent, structured way. They're great to work with on an individual basis because they make their teacher or tutor feel needed; tutoring an Abstract Random can give a teacher a real sense of accomplishment.

Concrete Sequential learners don't appreciate the Socratic method. They want to hear the truth from the wise man; they don't want to be pushed and prodded into discovering it on their own. Concrete Randoms love the Socratic method and learn well from it. A question has substance yet usually elicits a varied response; it is delivered to the learner as a concrete entity but it can be unpacked in a variety of ways. Abstract Sequential learners also like the Socratic method and are adept at synthesizing an open-ended question's range various answers. The Socratic method is usually a whole-class activity and, as such, engages Abstract Sequential learners less effectively.

Concrete Sequential learners like to read and analyze exemplary models of the kind of writing their teacher wants them to produce. They will analyze and synthesize the structure and style of the model, its syntax, the word order of its sentences, so they can imitate it effectively. Concrete Randoms are by nature less attentive to form and structure so they need exposure to model texts to remind them that readers appreciate a beginning, a middle, and an end. Abstract Sequentials read more for ideas than for form and structure. To them an exemplary reading does not so much model an imitable form as offer ideas and insights worth considering and perhaps integrating into their own work. Abstract Randoms would rather read a poem or a story than a model essay, but they need exposure to model compositions to help them learn how information can be, indeed must be, expressed and shaped in a way expected by the academic community.

Howard Gardner

The work of Howard Gardner also validates the need for an eclectic composition pedagogy. After studying, analyzing, and synthesizing much of the recent theory and research in human intelligence, Gardner came to the conclusion that there are nine different manifestations of human intelligence: Musical, Spatial, Mathematical, Linguistic, Intrapersonal, Interpersonal, Kinesthetic, Naturalistic, and Existentialist (Campbell, Campbell, and Dickinson). These intelligences are more than knacks, aptitudes, or proclivities. An intelligence, in Gardner's system, is a cognitive touchstone we use to help us perceive, process, organize, and understand knowledge, in short to help us make sense of our world. Each intelligence Gardner has identified has its own site within the human brain. The extent to which a learner possesses or is deficient in a given intelligence can be measured. Learners typically possess all of the intelligences to some degree, but each person will typically be very strong in two or three intelligences, average in some, and weak in others.

Students with strong verbal/linguistic intelligence can listen to and learn from a lecture. A lecture can also engage students with strong visual/spatial intelligence but only if the lecturer includes visual aids—charts, maps, pictures, film and video clips—in his or her presentation. Those high in interpersonal intelligence are expert empathizers, learners who try to and are good at understanding the perspective of others, so they, too, will try to attend to and learn from a lecture.

The interpersonally intelligent, however, work best in groups because they enjoy and are adept at working with others. If possible, a teacher should always try to make sure that each peer group includes a student high in interpersonal intelligence because such students encourage everyone to cooperate and stay on task. Because they are empathetic, they can accept criticism from others without feeling threatened, and they offer advice to other group members in a straightforward but diplomatic manner. The verbal/linguistic student also does well in a group but is more adept at offering than receiving advice about ways to improve the draft of a writing assignment.

Students high in logical/mathematical intelligence prefer the Socratic method because they love to solve problems, to pose and respond to questions. They love to experiment. Hillocks describes a teacher who distributed a sea shell to each of his students and had the students describe the shell in writing. The class then had to identify each sea shell, based upon the written description their classmates provided. Such an exercise appeals to students high in logical/mathematical intelligence while, at the same time, reinforces the importance of detail and precision in writing. Students high in bodily/kinesthetic intelligence would also enjoy the sea shell exercise because they need tactile, hands-on experience to learn effectively.

Writing teachers can tailor reading and writing assignments to intelligence types. The musically/rhythmically intelligent like to listen to, read, and write about music and love a multi-media assignment that allows them to include an audio component. Students high in bodily/kinesthetic intelligence like to read and write about sports, dance, anything that involves creative, coordinated movement. One writing teacher exploited a student's gift for mime by assigning a paper on that topic and by having the student, for a couple of extra points, demonstrate the art of mime to the rest of the class. Naturalistically intelligent students like to read and write about environmental issues and love it when a teacher sends them, journal in hand, into the woods to live and write like their hero, Henry David Thoreau.

The intrapersonally and the existentially intelligent are expert and natural journal writers, as well, because they love to reflect upon the significance of their personal experiences. They are sensitive and intuitive, philosophical and reflective. They tend to prefer their own company to the company of others so they are not forceful participants in peer conferencing sessions. They prefer to seek out their own knowledge rather than have it presented to them so they don't learn particularly well from a lecture. They like silent reading and tend to be good natural writers, especially adept at the personal narrative, creative nonfiction, and poetry.

Isabel Briggs Myers

The work of Isabel Briggs Myers also confirms the value of an eclectic composition pedagogy. Myers believes there are sixteen personality types, each type being the product of a combination of four pairs of contrapuntal human traits. We are either introverts or extraverts; we experience the world directly through our five senses or we rely more on our intuition to guide us; we think things through before we act or we act on our feelings and emotions; we act decisively and expeditiously or we procrastinate until we are comfortable with each aspect and possible outcome of a problem. Hamlet, for example, was an INTP, introverted, intuitive yet analytical, a procrastinator. Claudius was an ESTJ, extraverted, practical, smart in a cold and manipulative way, decisive in a selfish way.

A learning style is associated with each personality type. Extraverts like working in groups while introverts do not. Sensing learners like to be active, hands-on participants in each aspect of a structured learning process while intuitive learners prefer to step back, listen, philosophize, and let the big picture coalesce before them. Thinking learners like to apply the rules of logic to an issue, to debate, and to present an argument in writing. Feeling students value harmony and are the most effective peer conference participants because they can facilitate differences among group members. Judging students focus on the essentials and get the assignment done quickly, even if they have to ignore nuances. Perceptive learners consider nuance and will delay action until they have looked at an issue from all sides, until they have heard from everyone.

Myers' work indicates that personality type significantly influences life decisions, the decision, for example, as to which career to pursue. Engineering students are far more likely to be intuitive, rational, and decisive than practical, emotional, and compliant (Myers 41) while finance and commerce students are more likely to be more extraverted and practical than introspective and creative (Myers 42). Myers' work reveals the extent to which personality types and, hence, learning styles, differ among students selecting different majors or professional schools. Consider the implications of this for teaching first-year composition. First-year composition is a compulsory course at most colleges, and, consequently, the profile of a typical frosh comp class is going to be diverse, more diverse than most college classrooms are. As a rule, professors teach to groups of comparatively homogeneous students, who are likely to have similar interests and aptitudes and, hence, similar learning styles. They have—at least to a greater extent than we do—the luxury of limiting their number of teaching methods and of still being effective teachers. First-year composition is the academy's melting pot. We might have, in a class of twenty, a mix of business, engineering, humanities, social science, health science, fine arts students. First-year writing teachers—more so than their colleagues in other departments—need to recognize and respect the diverse ways of learning styles this array of students will utilize by practicing diverse ways of teaching.

Consider also the nature of writing as an academic discipline. Writing is a craft, a recursive cognitive process, and a social transaction. In a writing class, therefore, we both impart knowledge, develop skills, and guide students through a process. Written composition is not only an academic discipline in its own right, but also one that teaches a process necessary for success in virtually every other academic discipline. It is, arguably, the most difficult subject to teach. To teach writing effectively, a teacher needs to use an array of methods because effective writing requires competence in a wide variety of creative, social, and cognitive processes.

To make life easier for the writing teacher, should we segregate first-year composition courses according to interests or personality types or learning styles? There are advantages to doing so, and some universities do offer theme-based first-year writing courses. A writing teacher who focuses his or her first-year composition course on recent avant-garde movies will likely attract a class comprised mainly of introverted, intuitive, emotional, highly perceptive abstract random learners, high in visual and existential intelligence, and he or she will be able to tailor his or her teaching methods to his or her students' learning styles and intelligence types. On the other hand, freshmen need to learn how to learn. Introverts and concrete sequentials should learn how to adapt their personality and learning style so they can participate productively in group work—they will have to do so often as undergraduates and, eventually, as professionals. For the same reason, learners who are by nature intuitive, emotional, and introspective should learn how to adapt their personality and learning style so they can listen to and learn from a lecture. Students share the responsibility of realizing the goals of a writing course, and to do so they must be prepared to stretch themselves beyond their learning comfort zones.

Writing teachers, similarly, are charged with the responsibility of teaching **all** students—regardless of their personality, learning style, or dominant intelligences—to write competently. To discharge this responsibility, composition teachers need a variety of teaching strategies. Teachers need to lecture, facilitate group work, meet with their students alone, organize a debate, show a movie, arrange a field trip. No one method of teaching is likely to reach all students in a classroom as diverse in learning styles and intelligences as most first-year composition classes are. If writing teachers talk to each of their students alone and all of their students together; if they encourage students to write together and to write alone; if they teach students how to respond sensitively to each other's work and how to evaluate their own work independently; if they assign some topics and allow free choice for others; if they provide specific concrete instructions and encourage independent thinking; if they show movies, play music, ask questions, and present problems in need of solutions, they will connect with all their students and help all of them learn to write well.

Chapter Six
WHY ASSIGN READING IN A WRITING CLASS?

In addition to their handbook and their rhetoric text, writing students are usually required to purchase a reader, which typically contains well-written recently published articles from magazines and newspapers, usually about popular culture and current social and political issues. In fact, nationwide, reading anthologies are the most commonly-used textbook in first-year composition classes, more common than either handbooks or rhetorics (Stolarek 155). We want our students to read because we know we are better writers because we are avid readers. English teachers, even those with limited experience, find that the readers in their classes are usually the better writers. We feel intuitively that reading facilitates writing.

If intuition is a suspect criterion upon which to make decisions about curriculum, we can cite studies that validate our intuition. Heller tested the reading comprehension abilities of thirty-four college freshmen, then asked the students to write two in-class expository essays. She found that "at least 10 elements of written language were significantly related to the students' reading comprehension scores" (Abstract). Good readers wrote longer and more sophisticated sentences; poor readers were more prone to using coordination to join clauses together and wrote more run-on sentences. Using the Nelson-Denny Reading Test, Taylor measured the reading comprehension ability of 78 students enrolled in a community college English composition class. He compared the students' reading scores with their final grade and found a statistically significant relationship: better readers completed the composition course with higher grades. Valeri-Gold and Deming reviewed most of the college-level research on the reading/writing connection and found correlations between reading and writing abilities.

There are two related reasons why the text we process as readers influences the text we produce as writers. First, we learn by imitating the actions and behavior of those we admire, those who are already adept at the skill we are trying to acquire. Just as a budding basketball player might scrutinize the moves of a Kobe Bryant or a Tim Duncan, hoping to improve his game, so too might a budding writer scrutinize the wording and phrasing of his or her favorite writer, hoping that the ability to craft such fine sentences will rub off. The second reason has more to do with practicing a process than studying a product. Recent theory and research indicates that reading is not a passive and receptive, but an active and constructive process, similar in many ways to the writing process in that both use language to construct meaning. If we are reading a text properly—connecting its content to other texts we have read, aligning our minds with the author's, reflecting on what we are reading, re-reading one passage before we proceed to the next—we are cross training, indirectly learning how to write while processing what we read.

Prose Modeling

We do learn in part by imitating those who have mastered the skill we are trying to acquire, and so we expose students to good writing hoping there will be a rub-off effect, that students will work to emulate the form and style of accomplished writers. In a typical lesson in imprinting, the teacher insists students read the model closely and intently, then discusses with and asks students about the rhetorical strategies the writer is using and why they are effective. The editors of most composition readers include questions at the end of each reading, which the teacher might use to guide the lesson. Typically students are asked to identify the thesis of the model and to assess how the writer structures the information in the essay to develop its thesis. Students are directed to the essay's introduction and conclusion and asked to assess why they are effective. They are asked about the form and content of body paragraphs, about the manner in which the writer uses examples, details, definitions, comparisons, contrasts, causes, effects, and anecdotes to elucidate the paragraph's topic sentence. Together the teacher and the students examine the structure of individual sentences, noting how expert writers blend words, phrases, and clauses together to shape sentences that are energetic, rhythmic, varied in structure. This is what good writers do, the implicit message is, and this is what you should do, too.

There is research to support the efficacy of prose modeling. Hillocks conducted a meta-analysis of seven studies of the effect of prose modeling on writing performance and found a mean positive effect size, which measured the strength of the gain for experimental groups exposed to models over control groups not so exposed, of .22 (209). Charney and Carlson examined the effect of reading model Method sections of a social science report on students' ability to write a Method section and found that the experimental group exposed to the models wrote Methods sections that were better organized than those of control-group subjects who did not study models. Stolarek studied the effect of exposure to a model "modified chosisme" (157) on the ability to write in that same genre and found that prose modeling is effective pedagogy. Stolarek divided her subjects into five groups, the first of which was provided only with a description of a modified chosisme, the second of which was provided with a model only, the third of which was provided with both a description and a model, the fourth of which was provided with a model and an explication of the model, and the fifth of which was provided with a model, a description, and an explication. Students who were provided with the model supplemented by description and/or explication wrote significantly better modified chosismes than did students provided only with a description or only with a model. Stolarek suggests that description and explication of the model stimulated and invoked her subjects' metacognitive abilities and that it was this metacognitive awareness that lead to better performance.

Other compositionists, however, believe that prose modeling is only a marginally effective instructional strategy. Some advocates of the process-approach to the teaching of writing, for example, question the practice of assigning readings, when the intent is to encourage students to emulate the style and structure of the writer. They believe that knowledge of the components of the writing process (combined with the knowledge that these components are invoked recursively) is far more important than active reading is, for learning how to write well. Murray argues that product cannot teach process, claiming (though in a shaky analogy), that "The process of making meaning with written language cannot be understood by looking backward from a printed page [anymore than] a pig can be inferred from a sausage" (qtd. in Smagorinsky 163).

Hennessey agrees, claiming that the "greatest drawback of such models is their fundamental inability to illustrate the process of writing" (Abstract), which can be cultivated only through direct hands-on practice. Moreover, prose models in first-year composition readers may intimidate students, who despair that they will not be able to match the models' intellectual and rhetorical sophistication. Models do not develop a student writer's essential pre-writing skills, especially those abilities crucial to effective writing: assessing audience and establishing purpose. Nor is it easy to engage students in the process of examining the rhetoric of a written text, as parsing and diagramming sentences, unpacking paragraphs, and discerning structure are less than absorbing activities.

Some advocates of an expressivist pedagogy have also questioned the use of models. Expressivists stress personal writing and the cultivation of an authentic writer's voice that personal writing encourages. They feel that exposure to model compositions may contaminate and inhibit the development of the unique voice a good writer needs. Writers must develop their own style to develop their own voice, not imitate and co-opt the style, hence the voice of other writers. If models are used, they should come from students and be used to illustrate not a voice to emulate but the process by which voice is developed and refined (Elbow).

Even those researchers, the results of whose work is summarized above, came away from their studies uncertain about the pedagogical benefits of prose modeling. Considering a modest effect size of .22, Hillocks concluded that the study of models does not "have much impact on improvement in writing" (228). Reflecting upon the fact that their experimental group showed significant improvement in just one of four measures of effective writing (the ability to organize a Methods section), Charney and Carlson admit that "Taken as a whole the results indicate that models do not have automatic benefits for the writing process" (111). Stolarek's results are the most impressive, but her study is rather artificial. The modified chosisme is a completely prescribed two-paragraph text, the first paragraph of which is devoted, with "extremely detailed physical description" (172) to establishing the setting, the second of which is devoted exclusively to detailed action. It must use present tense in third person and be devoid of feelings, motives, and interpretations (172). As such, it bears no resemblance to the contents of a typical first-year composition reader. The insights the study offers into the importance of metacognitve awareness are interesting and pedagogically applicable. But the study offers little insight into the extent to which the study of model compositions in a typical composition reader will affect students' ability to write in a genre that is not identical to that of the model.

If we expect our students to become good writers because we guide them through a well-written text, pointing out as we proceed, what the writer has done well and how and why he or she has done it, we are likely to be somewhat disappointed. Theory and research suggest that prose modeling is a reasonable but hardly outstanding instructional strategy. But we should by no means expel the anthology of readings from the writing classroom. Reading engages students in a constructive, recursive, cognitive process that helps reify the writing process.

The Reading Process Recapitulates the Writing Process

The second and more compelling reason for assigning reading in a writing class is to engage students in a process that is similar to the writing process. Recent research in the reading/writing connection disputes the notion that reading and writing invoke different cognitive processes, that reading is passive and receptive, while writing is active and expressive. Like writing, reading is active and expressive; readers construct meaning while they read in a way quite similar to the way writers construct meaning while they write. Reading improves writing, not because readers imitate writers, but because reading provides practice in the process of constructing meaning with language.

Writing is a recursive process of reflecting upon a topic, planning, drafting, and revising. To use reading to improve writing, readers need to reflect upon the topic before they begin to read and while they are reading, establish a plan that will facilitate comprehension, "draft" the text they are reading by aligning themselves with the author, and revise their perceptions of the text as they reconsider its structure and content.

The title of a text, certainly its opening paragraphs, should activate a reader's existing knowledge of the text's subject and provoke the reader into reflecting upon that knowledge and how it might relate to the text he or she is about to read. Such reflection begins to establish a context for the information the reader is about to process, a context that will continue to evolve as the reader reads and reacts. In a similar way, a writer reflects upon his or her topic, plans and drafts in the context of that reflection, develops the draft and revises it as the composing process provokes new thoughts and refines others.

Writers plan before and while they write, considering ways, especially, of establishing a structure conducive to the development of the ideas, the main idea or thesis especially, of their text. Readers do something similar, as they root around in search of the structure upon which to hang the text's content, knowing how much structure assists comprehension.

Attentive readers, like good writers, create a first draft. As writers draft, they convey, in print, information that provokes additional, related information; as readers read, they seek cues that will help them "discover the upcoming meaning of the text," and from these cues "they hypothesize what is to follow" (Valeri-Gold and Deming 152). Tierney and Pearson explain this mirror image of the drafting processes of readers and writers, noting that

> what drives reading and writing is this desire to make sense of what is happening—to make things cohere. A writer achieves that fit by deciding what information to include and what to withhold. The reader accomplishes that by filling in the gaps . . . or making unsaid connections. (572)

To draft effectively, readers must align themselves with writers, just as writers must align themselves with their readers. Good writers, while they draft, keep the needs and expectations of their readers in mind and shape their text to best accommodate those needs and expectations. Good readers try to tap in to the author's point of view and to negotiate with the writer the meaning of the text.

Finally, proficient readers, like writers, revise text as they read. Good writers reconsider the structure of their work to make certain it most effectively conveys content; they reconsider content to make certain it fulfills the needs and expectations of readers and add to it if it does not; they reconsider their text's cohesion to make certain the text contains sufficient rhetorical signals to guide the reader's rhetorical journey. Readers, similarly, pause and reflect upon what they have read, and then they re-read and reevaluate segments of the text in the context of that reflection, and reassess, revise, and refine meaning. Like writing, reading is not a linear, but a recursive process.

We need to help our students read not only in ways that will encourage them to emulate good writing but also in ways that will facilitate their writing processes. Examining the effect that three canonical essays had on the writing of students in his undergraduate personal essay course, David Foster learned that student writing is affected more by students' ability to understand the process they undertake as readers than by any desire on their part to imitate the form, voice, and technique of better writers. He encouraged but did not require students "to adapt particular writing strategies and techniques from any of the readings for use in any of their essays" (521), and he discussed these strategies and techniques in class. "However, few students responded to the readings by incorporating text strategies into their essays—that is, by writing in the ways postulated in the 'models' rationale" (534). But the study turned Foster into a strong advocate of using readings in a writing class because his students

> described their readerly roles in deeply felt detail, and demonstrated these roles directly and often energetically in the specific *reading-to-write response* pieces. They made it clear that at least two of these pieces had expanded and deepened their sense of what good writers could do. (533–535)

Foster's students made little attempt to try to emulate the form, sentence structure, or voice of the model compositions. But reading benefited their writing because the models "expanded and deepened their sense of what good writers could do;" they reified the writing process.

Mariolina Salvatori goes further, arguing that students must not merely appreciate fine writing but engage actively and critically with a text, if authentic reading and writing abilities are to be nurtured. She criticizes "the enervated, atrophied kind of reading . . . immobilized within textbooks, and reduced therein to sets of disparate simplifying practices that . . . turn into meaningless and arbitrary exercises" (442) The questions editors include to guide comprehension and encourage imprinting "would foster nothing but 'canned' or 'theme' writing" (442). Drawing on the work of leading reading theorists, Salvatori recommends we implement instructional strategies that encourage students to articulate both a reflexive critique of a text and of themselves as readers as they respond to the text. She has her students write an initial response to a text, then write a reflective commentary on the process they went through as readers constructing meaning, and finally assess the efficacy of the text, as they have constructed it. By teaching students how to establish a responsible critical dialogue both with a text and with their own written response to the text, she tries to develop the critical mind and the facility with language that will help foster independent readers, whose independence will, in turn, nurture writing ability.

The work of Foster and Salvatori suggests that we should supplement questions designed to help students emulate good writing with strategies designed to help students improve understanding by asking them to reflect, in writing, upon their processes as readers. In this way, writing teachers execute a pedagogical double play, using reading to improve the writing process and writing to improve the reading process.

It helps that reading is an enjoyable pastime for many of our students. It is too easy to forget this, in the midst of an academic discussion on the pedagogical benefits of reading. Writing in his journal, one of my students reminded me of this, as he complained about having to monitor his reading process and look for ways to emulate the masters. "A baker," Alex analogized, "does not ask us to take one bite of cake to taste the sugar, another to taste the eggs, another, the flour. He just wants us to enjoy the whole cake experience." I took his point, but said, in my response, that if we are to bake our own cake, we do have to consult the recipes of experienced bakers. Furthermore, in the process of baking the cake, we'll probably learn things that will benefit us when we decide to bake bread. By all means, let them eat cake. But, for sound pedagogical reasons, writing teachers should assign as much reading, in a variety of genres, as students can reasonably process in the writing course they are taking. Good readers are good writers because they can seek in texts rhetorical strategies that are effective and, hence, worth emulating. Good readers are good writers because, as they read, they invoke processes similar to those writers use, as they construct meaning with language.

Chapter Seven
EFFECTIVE WRITING ASSIGNMENTS

A writing class should improve and develop students' writing abilities, engage students in the writing process, and teach students effective ways of presenting knowledge clearly, thoroughly, and accurately in a written text. In a composition class, then, the ideal writing assignment will engage students and motivate them to produce their best work, nurture their ability to write effectively, and expand and reify their knowledge of the content of the course. Given the range of interests, learning styles, and rhetorical sophistication students bring with them to the composition classroom, writing assignments that meet all of the criteria are difficult to design. But a writing prompt should help us meet at least one of the goals of the program.

Assignments That Develop Writing Ability

A good writing assignment not only helps us assess the degree to which students can process, understand, analyze, and synthesize the knowledge a course presents and the extent to which they can express this knowledge clearly, thoroughly, and accurately in writing, it will also help foster our students' writing abilities. Assuming practice does make perfect, any writing assignment should gradually and incrementally improve student writing. But certain assignments are especially valuable for targeting specific goals.

The standard writing assignment designed specifically to develop writing ability asks for a **revision** of a paper that a student has turned in and had assessed, if not graded. Since most first-year composition programs include instruction in the elements of the composing process, instructors do explain the revision process to students and usually reinforce instruction with end-of-chapter exercises that call for students to revise an ill-written passage. While such exercises have value, they should be supplemented with the more authentic exercise of asking students to revise their own work, perhaps rewarding them with a higher grade if the revision does improve the text. Despite instruction, "the very idea of revision . . . is alien" (Glenn, Goldthwaite, and Connors 97) to many students "who still see writing as a one-shot . . . event" (97). Asking students to revise in light of initial feedback from their instructor and/or their fellow students reinforces instruction especially in those components of writing process in which students may be deficient and reinforces, as well, the essentiality of revision to the composing process. Ideally, of course, students will gradually become independent revisers and the need for feedback on a draft—though it can always be helpful—will, at least, diminish.

Another assignment that targets the development of writing ability is the **sequence assignment**. There are two types of sequence assignment, one based on genre, the other on breaking down a complex topic into its component parts. Behind the **genre sequence assignment** lies the theory that it is easier for first-year students to write essays in some rhetorical modes than in others and that, if we start students off with the simpler mode and gradually advance to the more complex, we are implementing the "walk-before-you-can run" pedagogy, known to be effective and gradually building up their confidence as writers. Moffett's rhetorical continuum, for example, based upon the relationship of speaker/writer to subject, moves from narrative to exposition to argument (in Glenn, Goldthwaite, and Connors 87). Most English teachers agree that such a sequence does reflect a progression from comparatively simple to more demanding rhetorical modes.

Typically, then, a sequence assignment begins with a personal narrative because many English teachers believe this is the easiest rhetorical mode for students to handle. A personal narrative does not require research; it is comparatively easy to structure, since information is usually presented chronologically; and, because it uses first-person point of view, it requires a voice less formal and more accessible to novice writers than does a more academic assignment. Some English teachers are reluctant to ask for personal narratives from their students because such assignments can elicit personal information a student should not really share with a teacher, information that a teacher might even feel obliged to pass on to a college counselor. (Freeman 2; Morgan). But most English teachers agree that a carefully framed prompt can draw from students the kind of narrative that can build students' confidence as writers and help them develop their voice. A common assignment that requires a narrative asks students to describe a seminal experience that has helped shape the person they are today. Recently I read a great narrative, wherein the student described his gap-year experience, working as an assistant to an English-language teacher at a middle school in a poor part of Mexico City and then proceeded to explain how his values changed in light of this experience.

In a typical genre-sequence assignment, students next identify a central theme of their narrative and shape that theme into an expository essay, which presents information to readers in support of a thesis. My gap student, for example, followed his narrative with an essay, in which he compared and contrasted the curricula of a typical Mexican and a typical American public middle school. He focused his discussion on the attitudes, skills, and knowledge that a typical twelve-year-old Mexican and a typical twelve-year-old American student would acquire at school.

For the third and final phase of the genre-sequence assignment, students typically identify an aspect of their expository essay that could be shaped into a thesis for a persuasive essay, one that presents a cogent argument. Arguing effectively—especially in writing—requires the ability to think critically and to analyze and synthesize information, which are relatively sophisticated cognitive processes. Arguing effectively requires knowledge of and some empathy for opposing point of views, since an effective argument not only presents evidence in support of its thesis but also acknowledges and refute its antithesis. For his third assignment, my gap student made a case for less restrictive policies for Mexican students who want to attend university in America. True, his focus shifted from education to immigration, and far away from the personal experience which began the sequence, but, as long as the topic for the argument is related to the other topics in the sequence, the exercise should achieve its goals. Such a focus shift might also continue to motivate student writers who might tire of writing about the same topic, albeit in a different genre.

The genre sequence assignment also works very well for a writing-about-literature assignment. I begin by asking students for a personal response to a poem or story, to relate the poem or story to their own life experiences. Next, I ask for a written explication of the poem or story. Finally, I ask them to research other critical responses to the poem or story and to support the reading they find most accurate and informative. We can also request an argument based upon an issue the poem or story raises, especially if the work is so contemporary that it has not yet been subject to much critical analysis.

The other type of sequence assignment is the **component parts assignment**. Edward White believes complex writing topics should be broken down into component writing tasks that students should complete and turn in before they proceed to composing the whole essay. In other words, he argues for a sequence of writing assignments that build up to a major assignment. The compare/contrast essay, he notes, is a complex mode, requiring students to consider ways of juggling and synthesizing two different topics. Suppose, for example, an English teacher asked students to "Compare and contrast Shelley's 'Ode to the West Wind' with Wordsworth's 'Ode: Intimations of Immortality.'" Following White's method, the first-year composition teacher might subdivide the task into four separate assignments: 1) Write a summary and a review of "Ode to the West Wind"; 2) Write a summary and a review of "Ode: Intimations of Immortality"; 3) Compose an outline of similarities and differences between the two poem; 4) Write an essay in which you develop an idea about similarities and differences between the two poems. Presumably, all assignments would be worth marks, but the culminating assignment would be worth more than its subordinate writing tasks.

Similarly, students might write a better research paper, the culminating assignment in some first-year writing courses, if the teacher subdivides the task into several smaller writing assignments. White suggests students learn how to write a summary and to paraphrase a source before they begin a research paper because they typically have problems effectively incorporating information from secondary sources into their essays; they "simply insert quotations without comment or connections" (4). By summarizing and paraphrasing the source, students will understand it more thoroughly and will better know how to incorporate the information into their own work. This information must be cited, of course, so students should complete another assignment, which assesses their knowledge of the citation method the teacher has adopted.

Assignments That Motivate Students to Write

An effective writing assignment engages students in the writing process and motivates them to write, even to enjoy the experience. William Irmscher (in Glenn, Goldthwaite, and Connors 94) suggests that a writing assignment that has a clear and meaningful **purpose** will elicit better writing from students than one the purpose of which is vague, because a purposeful assignment motivates students to get started and sustains them as they work. There may be some value in asking students to summarize the plot of *The Scarlet Letter*, but such a topic is far less engaging than one that asks, for example, to explain the reasons why Hester refuses to reveal the identity of Pearl's father. The former topic is busy work; the latter urges students to grapple with more compelling issues that illuminate character and theme. It forces students to solve a problem in writing, a more demanding but also more rewarding assignment.

Some English educators believe we motivate students to write by letting them **select their own topics**, arguing that if they select their own topic, the topic will engage them and they will produce better work. Others disagree, supporting White's argument that selecting, defining, and refining a topic takes a lot of energy which students would better expend working on an essay their teacher has assigned (5). Moreover, White argues that topics which students have designed:

are more likely to reflect an unclear and problematic course design than a commitment to independent and creative thought; such topics are also an open invitation to the unscrupulous to purchase ready-made essays, which are widely available. (5)

Glenn, Goldthwaite, and Connors favor compromise, arguing that some students thrive with freedom of choice, while others prefer topics the teacher provides (84), a position that learning style theory also supports (Meyers-Briggs; Gregorc). If we prescribe some writing assignments and allow free choice on others, we accommodate both the free spirits who prefer to choose what they write about and the more cautious and grounded who prefer the security and certainty of a topic the authority figure has prescribed.

We can also motivate our students to write well by **presenting the topic** to them in a way that best stimulates their interest in it and that generates good writing. Intuitively, we may think that the more information we provide, the better our students will respond to the prompt. Students should produce better essays, for example, if we clearly specify the audience for whom the essay is to be written, suggest an appropriate tone or "voice" in which to speak, and carefully explain any key rhetorical terms we use, such as "analyze," "compare/contrast," and "classify." In fact, more is not necessarily better. James Williams, for example, argues that a prompt should specify context and purpose but should not be too detailed, because the "cognitive overload" of a too detailed assignment "inhibits writing performance" (288).

There is some research that confirms Williams' position. In a carefully designed study of placement-test essay topics, Brossell examined the effect on writing of topics presented to students at three levels of rhetorical specificity. Level 1 "provides a subject only, and that in abbreviated form" (170). "Level 2 supplies a subject and a brief orientation to it, but its context . . . does not demand conceptual restructuring" (170). Level 3 provides a complete rhetorical context, "information about purpose, audience, speaker, and subject" (170). He found that students given prompts at the second level of rhetorical specificity wrote longer and better essays than did students who received prompts at the first or third levels. In fact, the weakest essays came from the Level 3 students who were asked to assume a specific persona and write to a specific audience. Now these were placement test essays written in under an hour, and time constraints may have hindered students as they tried to process the heavy rhetorical demands of Level 3 topics. But it is also possible that the rhetorical demands of a prompt that specifies persona and audience complicate the assignment too much, overwhelm students, and actually confuse rather than motivate them.

In addition to the prompt itself, the assignment handout should include information about length, due date, and assessment criteria. The clearer we are about our expectations, the more we help motivate students to do their best work.

We can also use **whole-class discussion** to motivate students to do well and to keep them on track while they are writing. Even when the handout is perfectly clear, students appreciate the opportunity to ask questions about the instructions and the wording of the topics to make sure they start off on the right track. The discussion also works as a pre-writing exercise, in that it can provide students with some preliminary ideas they might eventually be able to work into their papers. It allows us an opportunity to stress those aspects of the assignment which need stressing, those points students might have misunderstood about the instructions on an earlier assignment.

If the assignment is a major paper which students have some weeks to complete, consider asking for brief weekly or bi-weekly oral progress reports. Students should report to the entire class, summarizing the progress they are making, indicating if they are having any problems, how they are conducting their research, what their thesis is. This activity helps maintain motivation and has several other advantages, as well. First, it monitors progress and helps prevent procrastination. Second, it establishes a tone of collaboration and team work. Students feel they are part of a composing community, and so notions about the social nature of writing are reinforced. Third, it can provide students with ideas about approaches to take, pitfalls to avoid, sources to check. Other students can offer advice: someone might know of a source his or her classmate might find useful. The teacher can monitor student progress, confirming that each student has a sound thesis and is in the process of assembling information to support the thesis.

Indeed, this approach has as many advantages for the teacher as it does for the student. It is, after all, a form of a student-teacher conference, and teachers rate such conferences as very effective ways to improve student writing (Freedman 78). The fact that it is a public conference does change its nature, making it more general and less personal. But what the individual student loses, the group gains by overhearing advice from which they might benefit, as well. This conference also helps the teacher to become familiar with the topic and the angle the student plans to take. Ultimately, it will be easier for the teacher to grade the assignments because he or she will be more familiar with their contents.

Assignments That Reify Knowledge About the Writing Process

Professors assign essays to help them evaluate the extent to which their students are mastering the content of their courses, the extent to which they are examining, reflecting upon, analyzing, and synthesizing the knowledge the professor is professing. This is, to be sure, sound pedagogy. In her landmark essay "Writing as a Mode of Learning," Janet Emig explains how and why writing reifies learning. The act of writing presupposes the implementation of one of the most important maxims of contemporary learning theory: to learn effectively, students must be active participants in the learning process. Students must be actively engaged when they process, interrogate, analyze, and synthesize information, as writing requires them to do. Moreover, the writing process animates both hemispheres of the brain, invoking as it does both the linear nature of the brain's left hemisphere and the creativity of the right. Writing reinforces what we learn because it provides the writer with an iconic product, in the form of print, which materially reinforces learning. Writing is connective; it incites the writer to connect segments of knowledge into a broader web of meaning. Finally, writing is self-paced, and we learn best when we work at our own pace. The thesis of Emig's essay is if you want your students to learn, get them to write. Writing reifies knowledge.

Learning outcomes for most college courses are prescribed and the writing assignments try to measure the extent to which students have mastered an aspect of the course's knowledge base, be it pre-Civil War American history, cellular biology, business management, Romantic poetry. For first-year composition, the knowledge base varies. Some colleges offer sections of first-year composition that focus on special topics—usually drawn from popular culture or current social issues—and they allow their students to choose a section focusing on a topic of interest to them. Some first-year composition programs focus on literature and students write interpretations, analyses, syntheses of the poems, stories, and plays on the syllabus.

But certainly most first-year composition courses at least include if not privilege the components of the writing process as the course's knowledge base, and, therefore, students should complete at least one writing assignment that displays their knowledge of the writing process. True, an essay assignment on the characteristics of an effective introduction for an expository essay or on methods of detecting and avoiding sentence fragments and run-on sentences or on five uses of the comma or on comparing and contrasting the MLA and the APA methods of citing sources or on recognizing and avoiding logical fallacies will not likely engage students as much as the current-social-issue or popular-culture topics. But the writing-about-writing assignment is one of the few that would achieve two of the three goals of a first-year writing program: It would develop and improve writing ability and it would reify the knowledge around which the course is, at least partly, based. Few teachers and fewer students would sanction more than one such assignment a term, and no writing teacher would abandon current-social-issue or popular-culture topics—staples in most first-year writing programs—in favor of writing assignments about punctuation rules or creative Internet research or citation methods. But the pedagogical benefits of the writing-about-writing assignment countermand its drudgery. Like the basketball player who endures the drudgery of a hundred sit-ups a day to improve his jump shot, the first-year writer should endure the drudgery of writing about the components of the writing process if the reward is worth the effort.

Another and perhaps more palatable take on the writing-about-writing assignment is the one that asks students to reflect upon their own growth and development as a writer. This assignment is usually required in programs that ask students to compile a writing portfolio. Teachers ask their students to include in the portfolio a letter which evaluates the quality of the assignments included in the portfolio, focusing especially on how the contents reflect the students' growth and development as writers over the term. It is an excellent assignment. Many programs, while recognizing their value, shy away from portfolio assessment because high workloads make it so difficult to monitor students as they compile their portfolios and to evaluate portfolios—especially those that include writing samples from other courses!—at the end of the term. The assignment can be adapted though, by insisting our students hang on to the work they have done for us, to re-read that work and our evaluative comments at the end of the term, and then to write a letter that presents their own assessment of their growth and development as writers (see White, "Scoring").

Students can have fun with this assignment, and it can be a rewarding one for the teacher when he or she reads comments such as this: "At first, I resented what you said about my first essay, especially that some of my paragraphs were 'anemic.' When I got over it and took your comments to heart, I resolved to add substance to my essays and I know my writing got better as a result." Not all assignments will be ones that students are eager to start working on, that foster their ability to write effectively, and that reify their knowledge of the content of the course. The interests and aptitudes of our students are simply too diverse. But if our assignments realize one or any combination of the three criteria for a good topic they can be allies in our effort to teach students how to write well.

Chapter Eight
TEACHING RESEARCH METHODS AND INVENTION STRATEGIES

College writing teachers often identify a lack of substance as one of the main problems with student writing. They express the concern in different ways: Student writing is "anemic"; it is not "robust"; it is "just too vague and superficial"; student writing "lacks insight" into the topics we assign. Clearly, one of our most important responsibilities as first-year writing teachers is to help students access knowledge and help them incorporate that knowledge into their written work so the ideas therein are developed to the extent expected in academic writing.

In most college courses much of the requisite knowledge comes from lectures, reading assignments, homework, projects, class discussion. As usual, first-year composition plays the maverick of the academy because in our first-year composition courses we assign essays on topics not necessarily central to the specific content of the course. We might, for example, ask our students to identify a major threat to the American way of life and (after narrowing the topic down to a workable thesis) to discuss in writing why this is a threat, how it became a threat, and how we might deal with it. But we do not have enough class time to explore terrorism, pollution, poverty, corporate malfeasance, crime, pornography, in any detail, and so we send them to the library, help them access authoritative and reliable Internet sources, and teach them some heuristics or invention strategies—methods of generating ideas about a topic—to help them acquire the information they will need to flesh out their work. This is not bad pedagogy, quite the reverse. By assigning topics students must research and reflect upon, we are encouraging independent research and critical and creative thinking, all of which help mold independent thinkers, a fundamental purpose of a college education.

Research

Some first-year writing programs draw a distinction between nonresearch and research papers and delay the library orientation module until later in the academic year, presumably because there are basics freshmen must learn before they take on the complex cognitive challenge of finding library sources. But research is one of the basics of composition pedagogy; a "basic" essay assignment, even a paragraph-length assignment, can be enriched through research. A narrative essay about what I did last summer is enriched if, instead of telling you there were thousands of people at Disney World the day he or she was there and they seemed to be from a variety of countries, your student does enough research so that he or she can tell you that on a typical weekday in mid-July, 33,000 people will visit Disney World, about 40 percent of whom will be tourists from other countries, including Great Britain, Japan, Germany, Mexico, and China. Since we teach, even in "basic" writing courses, that specific, concrete details and examples enliven writing, we must encourage students to find the information that will inform and enrich their work.

The ubiquity of the Internet is further reason why we should reconsider the old distinction between the research and nonresearch essay. Since our students can access information so easily now, from their own homes or from their college computer labs, it seems counterproductive to discourage students from doing research for a writing assignment. We do have to teach them how to evaluate Internet sources and to avoid those that are neither authoritative nor reliable, and many of them are not. Anyone who knows html can publish anything on the 'Net.

Your students need to know that a key clue to a website's trustworthiness is the last three letters of its Uniform Resource Locator. URLs that end in "gov" for government or "edu" for education are usually trustworthy since their point of origin is usually a university or a government agency. URLs for sites that end in "org" for organization are often biased. The website of the National Rifle Association (www.nra.org) would not be a good site to access to get unbiased information about gun control; the website of the Christian Coalition (www.cc.org) is not going to give you fair and reasonable information about school prayer. URLs for sites that end in "com" are commercial in nature and will often try to sell something, though there are reputable information sources, including the *New York Times* (www.nytimes.com) and the *Wall Street Journal* (www.wsj.com) that do end with these letters. URLs that end in "htm" are usually personal opinion Web pages, and they can be very biased and unreliable. Blogs, too, are suspect sources of the kind of information that might find its way into an academic essay.

When sources are used, they must be acknowledged. We would like to think we share, with our colleagues in other disciplines, the responsibility for teaching students how to avoid **plagiarism** by acknowledging sources using a recognized method, such as those developed and sanctioned by the Modern Language Association and the American Psychological Association. But just as we seem to be almost alone in teaching students how to conduct research, we seem to be alone in teaching citation methods. Traditionally, handbooks have included instruction in the MLA and APA methods of citing sources, though lately they have added the footnote method prescribed in *The Chicago Manual of Style* and the SCE method prescribed by the Council of Science Editors. The next chapter presents a comprehensive discussion of the plagiarism issue and discusses strategies we can use to deter it.

Invention Strategies

In addition to sending our students to the library and the Internet, where they can access the knowledge they need to flesh out their essays, we can teach them a few strategies that might enhance their ability to think creatively and thereby generate some ideas they can use in a writing assignment. Invention strategies or heuristics, as they are sometimes called, help students tap into some knowledge and insight they may not know they already possess and can help students find a focus for their writing and thereby facilitate the planning and first-drafting processes.

Considering audience, *a staple pre-writing exercise, is an excellent heuristic. Encourage your students to take time before they begin to draft to reflect upon and, in writing, respond to questions such as these:*

❏ Who is going to read and evaluate this work?
❏ What does my reader already know about this topic? Does he or she want me to include information I know he or she already knows?

❑ What will my reader not know about my topic? What will he or she expect to learn from me?

❑ How long does he or she expect my essay to be? How detailed should my information be, given the limits imposed by the word length my prof has specified?

By answering these questions, student writers often come up with ideas they might otherwise not have considered and they often find a way in to the topic, a starting point, a focus for their research, an antidote to the writer's block that afflicts so many freshmen writers.

Determining purpose, another staple pre-writing exercise, is another excellent heuristic. Encourage your students to answer, again in writing, these questions:

❑ Why am I writing this essay?

❑ What do I hope to accomplish?

❑ What rhetorical genre best serves my purpose and why?

The initial and broad response will relate to the third question, as students confirm the nature of the assignment's rhetorical mode. In most cases the purpose will be to present information (the expository mode) or to present an argument (the persuasive mode), though, occasionally students will be asked to write a personal narrative. Written responses to the other questions, especially the second, will help student writers focus their research and begin to establish the form, the structure their essay will take.

Profiling readers and establishing purpose can be used as effective **freewriting** prompts. Freewriting is that process of writing, uninterrupted, for a set period of time, about a given prompt in order to generate information about the topic implicit in the prompt. Focused freewriting exercises, usually no more than fifteen minutes long, help students overcome writer's block, develop a plan, and find some of the content they will need to complete the assignment successfully. Refinements to the freewriting process can further the same goals, especially those related to planning and structuring writing. **Webbing or clustering**, for example, is a pre-writing exercise wherein the writer jots down phrases related to his or her topic then circles them and connects related phrases together in order to discern connections between them. Webbing can facilitate planning and generate content for solid paragraph development.

Freewriting is probably the most widely used invention strategy in the composition classroom. Peter Elbow is among the leading exponents of the benefits of freewriting. Elbow recommends students freewrite at least three times a week and that teachers never grade their students' freewriting. Freewriting is only effective if it is unconstrained and, faced with the prospect of a grade, students will likely sacrifice spontaneity to neatness and correctness, believing their grade will be higher as a consequence.

Some English educators recommend freewriting be done in stages. During the first stage, the writer freewrites for, say, ten minutes, then stops, reads over what he or she has written, and circles or underlines the phrase, sentence or passage he or she deems to be most significant. Then, using that phrase, sentence, or passage as the prompt, the writer freewrites again, perhaps for a reduced length of time. This process can be repeated, until the writer feels his or her stored knowledge and creative energy are tapped out. Murray recommends students freewrite on index cards, not for a set period of time but just until one side of the card is filled. The key idea is the prompt for the student to use as he or she fills the other side of the card. "The index cards help students scrutinize their writing in small chunks for good ideas" (in Soven 35).

Rai Peterson argues that freewriting helps students overcome the dreaded writer's block. Indeed, by its very nature, freewriting forbids writer's block because it forces students to be productive, to generate at least some text in a short period of time. "Once students have something on paper," Peterson argues, "they will more easily relax and take risks in composing lively discourse" (34). For Peterson, freewriting is "an amazingly productive prewriting activity" (34).

Connors, Goldthwaite, and Glenn claim that freewriting loosens "the inhibitions of the inexperienced writer" (224). They claim that most proponents of freewriting have their students freewrite for a few minutes at the beginning of every class, "for at least four or five weeks of the term" (226). Such prolonged experience with freewriting "demystifies the writing process" (226). It convinces students that everyone, not just the linguistically gifted, can write, and it helps them appreciate the difference between writing and editing. Writing is a creative act demanding the free flow of ideas freewriting fosters. Editing is the application of rules to written discourse. It is not, like freewriting, a pre-writing activity, but one undertaken while a writer drafts and redrafts his or her work.

Not all English educators are champions of freewriting. George Hillocks Jr. reviewed ten empirical studies on the efficacy of freewriting and combined their findings and results using a sophisticated statistical procedure known as a meta-analysis. Hillocks found that the writing of experimental group students who used freewriting did improve more than their control group counterparts who did not, but the improvement was modest. Even "a steady diet of free-writing (daily or several times per week), Hillocks notes, "does not accomplish what its proponents hope for" (178) But, generally speaking, experienced writing teachers support freewriting as an instructional strategy, believing that the class time they allot to freewriting helps students produce more robust written assignments.

Most students, after they have done some research and some freewriting assessing audience and determining purpose are ready, maybe even eager, to begin drafting, and they tend to be reluctant to give up writing time to try out further invention strategies. But should they feel the need to explore an issue further before they begin to draft, there are other reputable and widely used heuristics they can try, some based upon ancient, some on sophisticated contemporary rhetorical theory. Among the best known are Aristotle's *topoi*, Kenneth Burke's dramatistic Pentad, and Kenneth Pike's Tagmemics.

Aristotle's *topoi* are a collection of prompts writers can use to help them generate the arguments they need to support a thesis. Aristotle's work implies, for example, that, by defining their terms precisely, by drawing analogies that compare an aspect of a topic to other entities or phenomena, by reflecting upon the consequences of actions and events, and by considering the "testimony" of experts, writers can generate a wide range of ideas that might enrich and inform their work (Glenn, Goldthwaite, and Connors 206–211). Suppose, for example, a student wanted to argue that the Federal Communications Commission should monitor more closely special-event television programs that draw millions of viewers and should impose stiff penalties if lewd and offensive acts are broadcast during such programs. By carefully defining "lewd and offensive" and "stiff penalties," by comparing the offensive act to similar societal transgressions, by reflecting upon the consequences such acts might have on younger viewers, and by referencing the testimony of psychologists, politicians, and ministers sympathetic to his or her point of view, your student would generate arguments and support for arguments which would elucidate his or her thesis.

Burke's Pentad (fully explained in *A Grammar of Motives*) is a series of five conditions and circumstances, originally designed as a method for understanding and interpreting human responses to specific situations and, hence, widely used in literary analysis. But compositionists have also appropriated the Pentad and adapted the questions each of its five circumstances presuppose as a useful heuristic. The five conditions and circumstances are the act, the scene, the agent, the agency, and the purpose. A variety of questions emerge from the conditions, the obvious ones being

❑ What act occurred?
❑ Where did the act happen?
❑ Who acted?
❑ How did the agents act?
❑ Why did they act?

Apply these questions to our thesis that asserts that the FCC needs to be more proactive to control television smut, and you can see that a student writer might, indeed, gain insights he or she can use to augment his or her argument. The Pentad can improve a written text, in that it urges writers to establish, clearly and precisely, the nature of an action, its context, and the motives of those who initiated and continue to drive it.

Pike's Tagmemics (fully articulated in *Rhetoric: Discovery and Change*) is a complete and complex theory of discourse, one aspect of which is the "tagmemic discovery matrix," which some writing teachers have found useful as a way of helping students generate ideas and insights about a given essay topic. Pike believed that we can come to understanding of the true nature of an event, object, or concept if we examine that event, object, or concept from a variety of perspectives and under a variety of conditions. The perspectives are as an entity in itself, a "particle"; as a process or "wave"; and as part of a system, a "field." The conditions are "contrast," which assesses the uniqueness—as a particle, wave, and field—of the event, object, or concept under study; "variation," which determines the point at which uniqueness vanishes; and "distribution," which considers the relationship of the event, object, or concept, to the larger system of which it is a part. Pike's matrix, then, is nine-fold, assessing as it does, the contrast, variation, and distribution within the context of each particle, wave, and field. Applying Pike's matrix to our thesis about FCC censorship would force us to consider a lewd incident as an act in and of itself, its nature, the adjustments needed to render the act acceptable, the prevalence on television of similar acts, the prevalence in other media of similar acts, the process under which the act unfolded to render it unacceptable, the point at which it became lewd, the broader societal issues the frequency of such acts raises. A student writer who undertakes such an exercise would likely discover ideas and insights he or she could incorporate into an essay that argues for increased FCC vigilance.

Constructing a tagmemic discovery matrix is challenging and time consuming and the rewards may not be worth the effort if simpler invention strategies, especially the freewritten responses to questions about audience and purpose, have wrung dry the well of invention. But if your students have considered audience and determined purpose and still do not have sufficient insight into their topics to begin drafting, if they complain still of writer's block, if they are writing on an especially complex topic, or if they are in need of creative solutions to rhetorical problems, they can always turn to Aristotle, Burke, and Pike for additional help.

Chapter Nine
HOW TO PREVENT PLAGIARISM

For first-year writing students, the Internet is technology's double-edged sword, a phenomenal source of instantly accessible information but one from which it is very tempting to pilfer. Recent studies confirm what many of us have suspected: plagiarism is on the rise because the Internet is home to scores of paper mills, from which students can easily purchase ready-to-submit essays on a vast array of topics, and home, as well, to billions of pages of freely available text from which students can easily cut selected information and paste it into a writing assignment. The most comprehensive and widely cited study was done in 2003 by Rutgers University professor Donald McCabe, who surveyed some 18,000 undergraduates at twenty-three schools and found that 38 percent of these students admitted to downloading information from the Internet and including that information, unacknowledged, in a writing assignment (Rimer).

It is true and something of a relief to learn that formal documented charges of plagiarism submitted to college committees responsible for maintaining academic integrity are still rare. My Lexis-Nexis search revealed that at Indiana University in Bloomington, Auburn University, and the University of Wisconsin, Madison, all large schools with populations of anywhere from 25,000 to 40,000, fewer than 150 cases of plagiarism are reported (per school) in a year, while at Princeton, a school of some 7,000 students, about 20 cases are reported each year. But while we are, understandably, reluctant to bring formal charges against our students and jeopardize their future, we still must confront and curtail the growing plagiarism problem. This chapter presents three methods of doing so. From the most to the least desirable, they are:

- ❏ educate students so they know exactly what plagiarism is, why it is wrong, and what they must do to prevent it;
- ❏ design writing assignments in a way that makes it difficult for students to use outside sources without acknowledgement;
- ❏ inform students who you suspect have submitted plagiarized work that you will be vetting that work through an anti-plagiarism software program.

Explain and Discuss the Issue

A recurring theme in recent articles about student plagiarism asserts that students do not really know what plagiarism is. Certainly, they know that purchasing an essay from an Internet paper mill or copying directly from a book is cheating. But they are less certain about cutting a passage or two from an Internet source and pasting it into their paper and less certain about citing information that they have paraphrased from any source.

Fortunately, instances of plagiarism do decrease, once students understand the nature of the problem. One study compared student attitudes in English classes, where teachers did educate students about plagiarism, with classes wherein plagiarism was not discussed. About 40 percent of the students in the latter classes expressed the belief that copying from the Internet was acceptable, compared with about 23 percent of the students in the former classes, a statistically significant difference ("Teaching About Plagiarism" 1).

The place to begin to educate students about plagiarism, how to avoid it, and what the consequences will be for committing it is on your course syllabus. Your syllabus needs a section on plagiarism, a section that clearly and thoroughly defines the terms, explains the rules, and outlines the punishment when those rules are violated. Here is an example:

Plagiarism is a form of theft that occurs when one writer copies the words or appropriates the ideas of another writer without acknowledging that writer as the source of those words and/or ideas. Instead, the plagiarist is attempting to create the impression that the work of another is his or her own original work.

If, in a written assignment, you use the written words, the data, and/or the written ideas of another writer, you must acknowledge the author of that information. If you fail to acknowledge the fact that you have used the words, data, and/or ideas of another writer in your own written text, you are guilty of plagiarism. Note that plagiarism is not limited, as students sometimes think it is, to copying a passage from a source word for word. If you acquire specific information from a source, you must acknowledge that source, even if you have used you own words and paraphrased that information. Note, as well, that copying the work of another student or any other unpublished source also constitutes plagiarism.

There are a variety of acceptable ways of acknowledging the work of other writers. Your instructor will discuss this issue with you in more detail and will teach you one or two acceptable methods of citing sources in academic writing.

If, in any of your assignments, you do plagiarize the work of another writer, the **minimum penalty** your instructor will impose will be a failing grade for that assignment. If, in the judgment of your instructor, the plagiarism was unintentional, he or she may allow you to re-write the assignment. If, in the judgment of your instructor, the plagiarism is flagrant (if, for example, the entire paper has been copied word for word from a source), or if it is a second offense, you may fail the course. Instructors are also required to report instances of plagiarism to the Director of the Writing Program or the Chair of the Department, who may, in turn, report the case to the University's Office of Judicial Affairs.

If you review this section in the first week of classes and review it every time you present a new writing assignment, discuss the policy with students, and respond to their questions and concerns about the issue, you should see fewer plagiarized papers.

Margaret Price, however, argues that it is not enough merely to include a plagiarism policy in your syllabus and remind students of it when you give them an assignment, because plagiarism is contextual and difficult to define:

> What we think of as plagiarism shifts across historical time periods, across cultures, across workplaces, even across academic disciplines. We need to stop treating plagiarism like a pure moral absolute . . . and start explaining it in a way that accounts for these shifting features of context. (90)

To illustrate her thesis, she critiques the written plagiarism policies of two university English departments and one English professor, pointing out that their use of such terms as "common knowledge," "your own work," and even "fact" are context dependent (92–93). She recommends a policy that admits "that citation is a convention, and conventions shift across time and locations" (106). She recommends, as well, that our plagiarism policy contains blank spaces preceded by "prompts for students to write in ideas or questions" (107) in order to help students clarify difficult parts of the policy.

The Plagiarism-Proof Writing Assignment

Search engines are so powerful now that students can find information, if not a complete paper, about virtually any topic. But we can frame topics in a way that will at least make it harder for students to purchase a ready-made essay. We can also rely a little bit more on in-class writing assignments. And, most important of all, we can teach writing as a process and guide our students through the components of the process by reviewing drafts and outlines and questioning them about the sources they are using.

One of my colleagues, in her first-year persuasive writing course, distributes three mini-sized candy bars to her students, asks them to choose the one they would select as the official candy bar of their section of English 100, and assigns a 1,500-word persuasive essay in which they must defend their selection and explain why the other two did not make the grade. I Googled "snickers three musketeers and twix" and got 682 hits in 0.10 seconds. I got lists of favorite candy bars, warnings about peanut allergies, information about the corporations that manufacture these products, advertisements for these products, and exhortations to purchase them, but no paper mill essays on the topic or really much other information from which students could plagiarize. Topics like this one my colleague assigns fulfill the requirements of the course, are fun, and preclude or at least hinder cheating. With a bit of imagination, we should be able to assign at least one paper on a topic that fulfils the goals of our course but is framed in such a way as to make plagiarism difficult.

The plagiarism crisis also increases the importance of the in-class writing assignment. We provide instruction in and assign in-class essays because the ability to write extemporaneously is an important skill we want to help our students develop. The in-class assignment has also helped us identify English-as-a-second-language students and, if necessary, to reassign them to a more appropriate class. We have also used in-class essays to establish a style benchmark for each of our students to help us compare their in-class with their out-of-class writing. If the style of their take-home assignments is obviously more sophisticated than their in-class ones, the plagiarism alarm bell goes off and we do some investigating to determine if the better style is the result of the extra time students had to complete the assignment or the result of outside help. The Internet has certainly increased the style-benchmark justification for the in-class assignment.

We can also control plagiarism by monitoring the progress of students as they work their way through a writing assignment, as many writing teachers, committed to the process approach to teaching writing, do now as a matter of course. If students have, say, ten days to complete an assignment, they can submit, at two- or three-day intervals, an outline, a draft, an annotated bibliography, and a second draft, before they submit the finished product. True, this is labor-intensive intervention that still may not deter the most determined cheaters. But it will deter most, and, in keeping with the educational zeitgeist that sees the role of the teacher as a coach, collaborator, guide, and mentor, it is the most pedagogically sound way of handling the problem.

The Plagiarism Detection Software Program

There may be some students who succeed in breaking apart a published essay, students who duly submit an outline and a draft they have not written and who can talk convincingly about the sources they pretend to have accessed. There may be times when our workload makes it impossible to check drafts, outlines, and sources before an essay is due. And certainly it is not always possible to design a writing assignment immune or even resistant to the wiles of a plagiarist. But what we still can do, if we receive a suspect essay, is to vet that essay through a plagiarism detection program.

It is only right that we tell a student who we suspect has submitted plagiarized work that we plan to vet that work through such a program, to give the student a chance to confess, apologize, and make amends. Price is surely right in condemning the "gotcha!" attitude of some teachers.

Moreover, we must proceed cautiously, even if we do find some evidence of plagiarism. Anti-plagiarism programs vet student essays through a system that contains billions of pages of electronic text. TurnItIn.com, the most widely used database, checks student papers against not only the Internet, but also other texts previously submitted to the system and against the Pro-Quest database, which stores the contents of hundreds of periodicals. A database so powerful will likely catch many cheaters, but it may falsely accuse some innocents as well. The odds that a student will compose a sentence identical to one in a billion-page database are not insignificant. When the presenter at the TurnItIn.com workshop I attended typed, extemporaneously, a paragraph about the business hours of the university's Instructional Resources Technology Center and vetted it through the system, the system found and duly color-coded a nearly identical sentence. In these litigious times, students and parents will not suffer gladly false charges of academic misconduct.

There is, potentially, another legal quandary associated with plagiarism detection services. An essay submitted to a service automatically becomes included in its data bank. Those essays are the intellectual property of the writers, but their work is not recognized, not, ironically, cited by those who own and operate the service. Nor, of course, are writers compensated for their work, though they are helping corporations such as iParadigms, which owns TurnItIt.com, get rich.

Some programs place the onus on students and insist that, before they submit their work for grading, students provide proof that they have vetted their work through an online plagiarism program, usually one for which the university has an onsite license it has had to purchase. But there are serious limitations to this practice, as well. It is a subtle but nevertheless real form of electronic surveillance, and, if it does not violate the presumption of innocence, it at least denies students the benefit of the doubt. There is a danger, as well, that we will foster an atmosphere of distrust which can adversely affect the tone of the classroom and which is antithetical to the values of a liberal-humanist education, which rejects the teacher-as-rule-enforcer model, in favor of one that encourages at least some sharing of power between students and teachers. The electronic plagiarism check actually cedes some power and authority to a machine, a distasteful prospect, certainly to many professors in the liberal arts, humanities, and social sciences.

We need to remember, finally, that there are billions of pages of text students have access to but that are not in the databases anti-plagiarism programs monitor. Nor can these programs—at least, not yet—zap roommates, friends, siblings, parents, aunts, uncles, or cousins who have written some or all of a friend's or a relative's paper. Anti-plagiarism software monitors only a portion of the resources to which ethically challenged students have access.

Plagiarism detection software programs should be used sparingly by teachers who have a compelling reason to believe they have received unoriginal work and only after the teacher has discussed the problem with the student and told him or her of the action that will be taken. As the national Writing Program Administrators' statement on plagiarism makes clear, the availability of plagiarism detection services "should never be used to justify the avoidance of responsible teaching methods" ("Defining and Avoiding Plagiarism"). Fortunately, the need for such services diminish markedly when students are informed: when they recognize what plagiarism is, know how to prevent it, and understand the consequences for violating the plagiarism policy.

Chapter Ten

TEACHING STUDENTS HOW TO REVISE THEIR WRITING: THE "4S" METHOD

Revision is the process of making alterations and improvements to a piece of written discourse at the overall structural and/or paragraph levels. It is distinct from its rhetorical cousin, editing, which is the process of making changes and corrections to the words and/or sentences within a piece of writing. Revising is a recursive process; it is not a final or penultimate stage in the creation of a written text; writers usually revise their work as they write a draft, not only after a draft is done. Writers revise to clarify the purpose, the thesis of their text. They revise in search of the best way to impose an order and structure onto their work, an order and structure that will best help readers follow along and understand the content of the text. They revise to make that order and structure clear to their readers. They revise to add the information—the examples, details, definitions, comparisons, contrasts, causes, effects—their readers need to comprehend the texts they are creating. They revise to remove the information readers would find superfluous. Writers undertake all aspects of the writing process for the benefit of their readers—to make their texts "reader friendly"—but no component of the process is more selfless than revision.

In a first-year composition classroom, the ability to revise writing effectively separates the girls and the boys from the women and the men. Mature writers, as a rule, edit <u>and</u> revise their work; immature writers, as a rule, edit but give revision short shrift. In their study of revising practices, Flower et al. found that beginning writers were more inclined to proofread than revise their texts. Any inclination to revise they might have had was stymied because they had no clear sense of what the thesis, the "gist," of their text was. They had trouble detecting sections of their texts in need of revision, and, when they did realize where changes were needed, they had trouble assessing the exact nature of the problem and implementing the required revisions. Successful writers, on the other hand, composed texts that had a clear purpose, a goal to achieve, and, when they revised, they did so to clarify and enhance and thereby reach that goal.

Studies by other compositionists have reached similar conclusions. Nancy Sommers examined the revision strategies of student writers and experienced adult writers. She found that student writers are more concerned with changing the words in a draft than in adding content or in reshaping existing content. When they did revise, they tended to restrict revision to their opening paragraph. Richard Beach, similarly, found that weaker writers tended not to revise for content, while stronger writers revised to clarify their thesis and to reconsider the need to develop ideas in more detail. Robert Yagelski examined the editing and revising strategies of twelfth-graders and found that surface changes accounted for 81.7 percent of the changes they made to their texts, while substantive structural and content changes accounted for only 18.3 percent of the changes they made. Experienced writers, on the other hand, tend to change the structure, add to the content, and clarify the ideas of an early draft. Student writers often seem unaware of the need to change the big picture in ways that help the reader see it.

Why are student writers reluctant to revise their work? It is partly because students too often equate correct writing with good writing: as long as there are no errors in grammar, spelling, and punctuation, they reason, their work will be good, and the teacher will be happy. It's partly because word processing programs, whose spell and grammar checks are, at least, somewhat helpful in editing, do not offer effective programs to help students revise. It's partly because revision is hard work, demanding the metacognitive ability to reflect critically on work in progress and to alter that work in the context of that reflection. And it's partly because we lack simple but effective instructional strategies that will encourage students to revise and provide them with some basic guidelines for doing so.

The aim of this chapter is to present a simple revision taxonomy that alerts students to the importance of revision and provides them with an easy-to-remember framework for beginning and sustaining the revising process. It is a "4S" taxonomy, the S's representing the four components of the revising process: structure, substance, sequence, and style. I stress "components" and not "stages" because the revising process is recursive and because writers often work with two of the components—substance and style, for example—concurrently.

Structure

Students should revise their written work to tighten its structure, to make certain each paragraph supports, elucidates, develops their thesis. A sound structure enhances clarity and readability; a random or rambling structure enhances ambiguity, a virtue for a poem, perhaps, but not for a college essay.

Explode early the myth that the writing process involves filling out a plan developed during the pre-writing stage. Planning is an important part of pre-writing, but a pre-written plan is clay not granite and will be re-shaped as the writing process unfolds and takes the writer places the plan did not anticipate. A pre-written plan is useful in that it provides some guidance and some substance, but plans change as writers cast the points of the plan into sentences that provoke new ideas the pre-written plan did not anticipate. Encourage your students to make an outline of their work not only before they write but also <u>after</u> they believe their text is complete and ready to be turned in. It is at this point—the point where writers believe their work is over—that an outline will reveal structural flaws that need to be corrected with another round of revision. A writer should have some idea where he or she is going before his or her journey begins but must know exactly how he or she got there when it ends.

I will endorse, here, at least in a limited way, assigning the infamous five-paragraph theme, as a way of alerting students to the importance of structure. With its clear thesis at the end of the first paragraph, its three paragraphs to elucidate the thesis, and its concluding paragraph to summarize the body and reaffirm the thesis, the five-paragraph essay reminds us of the relationships among meaning, clarity, and structure. It is widely condemned because it is artificial, it constricts the creativity important to the writing process, and it is anomalous, existing as it does only in writing classes for beginners. Its detractors have a point and college freshmen should soon move beyond its confines to more complex writing assignments. But if it has pedagogical value, it should not be condemned simply because it is not a genre within which journalists, academics, and other professional writers work. Concert pianists don't play the scales in public, but they were an essential part of their apprenticeship, and their public performances are better for having learned them.

Substance

Urge your students to check each paragraph of their drafts to make sure they contain the examples, details, comparisons, contrasts, definitions, causes, effects, anecdotes readers will require to understand completely the points the essay is making. I tell my students the old joke about a traveling salesman who went into a pet store in Costa Rica and found there a bird that could speak eight different languages. The bird cost $10,000, but he had to buy it as a gift for his mother who was a linguistics professor. So he sent his or her the bird with a letter that read: "Dear Mom: I know how much you are going to enjoy this bird." Two weeks later, the salesman received his mother's reply: "Thank you. You were so right. I did enjoy the bird. It was delicious." The salesman failed to revise his letter, failed to explain or elaborate on the crucial infinitive "to enjoy" and—literally—paid a high price for his rhetorical incompetence.

Lack of substance is especially problematic in the paragraphs in the body of student essays. The conventions for effective introductions and conclusions are generally straightforward. The introductory paragraph (or introductory discourse bloc, in a longer paper) needs, basically, to engage the reader and present the thesis. The concluding paragraph (or concluding discourse bloc in a longer paper) needs to reaffirm the thesis and establish a sense of closure. Students may have problems with introductions and conclusion but lack of substance is not usually one of them.

Students need some strategies so they can, first, recognize an underdeveloped body paragraph when they re-read it and, second, revise it to give it the substance it needs. As we learned in Chapter 10, the average paragraph in a good first-year essay is about 132 words long, so your students should be on alert if they have paragraphs shorter than that average. These paragraphs won't necessarily be underdeveloped, but their less-than-average length marks them as paragraphs that need a second look.

Having determined that a paragraph lacks substance, student writers need strategies to develop that paragraph in more detail. Since a paragraph might lack substance because it does not have a clear topic and, hence, has nothing upon which to hang needed information, instruction in revising for substance begins by explaining to students that a body paragraph needs a topic sentence. The topic sentence might be implied, often is, in fact, in effective writing, as researchers who have studied the frequency and placement of topic sentences have discovered (Braddock). But even if implicit, the paragraph's topic must be clear enough that a student writer could express it in a single sentence, even if he or she chooses not to include that sentence, word for word, in the paragraph. Once the student identifies the topic sentence, implicit or explicit, he or she can reflect upon the information necessary to elucidate the topic to the extent readers need to grasp its meaning and implications, then add the details, examples, definitions, causes, effects, comparisons, contrasts, and anecdotes readers need and expect.

It is true that neophyte writers need reader feedback while they are revising because they lack that radar experienced writers have that alerts them to an inadequately developed paragraph. The peer and/or teacher conference (discussed in detail in Chapter 12) that focuses on revising a draft of a writing assignment is effective in helping students identify and develop anemic paragraphs. Another great pedagogical strategy is to share with your students successive drafts of one of your own pieces of writing, one, especially, that needed to be revised to make it more substantial. Talk about how you determined the need for additional content and how exactly you revised your text to make it more substantial.

Sequence

While revising their work, students need to consider the sequence within which their paragraphs and sentences are arranged and presented. Effective writers use cohesive ties to establish clear and logical sequencing between and among the sentences within a paragraph and between and among the paragraphs within the text as a whole. Research indicates that better writers use more of these cohesive ties than less skilled writers do (Witte and Faigley). A sound structure certainly helps create the impression that the paragraphs within a text are sequential. But an effective text will have other cohesive signals, within paragraphs, to clarify relationships between and among sentences and so guide readers smoothly along the journey on which the text is taking them.

There are essentially three kinds of cohesive signals, based upon the important rhetorical principles of transition, repetition, and substitution. Transitional words and phrases, such as but, on the other hand, moreover, for example, however, and in addition signal readers that the writer will contradict or elaborate upon the subject of the previous sentence or, if the sentence is the first in the paragraph, the previous paragraph. Writers often repeat a key word, or a variation of it, to establish cohesion within a paragraph. In the paragraph before this one, for example, the word "sequence" is in the first sentence; the word "sequencing" is in the second sentence; and the word "sequential" is in the fourth sentence. Since too much repetition is a solecism, writers often achieve cohesion by using a synonym for, or a pronoun in place of, a key word.

The rhetoric or handbook your program uses will likely discuss, in some detail, cohesive ties and how student writers should use them to improve their work. Given the indispensable role cohesive ties play in the construction of a well-ordered and sequential text, this is an important chapter to cover thoroughly. Call attention, as well, to the ways in which the authors of the model texts you read and discuss in your class use cohesive ties to maintain the order and flow of their essays.

Of course, students need to recognize a lack of sequence in their own writing before they can revise to improve that text's cohesion. Peers and teachers reviewing a draft of a student's work will often spot places where the text's cohesion needs to be tightened, especially those places the writer misses because he or she knows the text so well he or she makes the transitions subconsciously and forgets to add them for the benefit of his or her readers. Also encourage your students to read their work aloud as they revise; when a writer hears his or her text, he or she will often find places where transitions need to be tightened, places he or she would miss during a silent re-reading. Indeed, the read-aloud is a most effective strategy for discerning weaknesses not only in the sequence of a text but in its structure, substance, and style, as well.

Style

Finally, insist your students revise their written work to reconsider and, if necessary, improve its style. Style is the image a text presents, the way in which it is turned out, how it is dressed. Like style in clothes, style in writing can be formal, informal, slovenly, whimsical, hip, retro, appropriate, inappropriate, athletic, gothic, or punk, depending, as usual, upon the writer's purpose and context and the needs and expectations of his or her readers. Reflecting on the efficacy of their style, then, our students need to make certain the style of their text suits its purpose and is appropriate for its audience. Usually, in a first-year composition class, this equates to an academic essay that presents information to or develops an argument for an English instructor.

Specific strategies for helping students recognize a good style are covered in detail in Chapter 13. Briefly, freshmen with a robust writing style use subordination effectively to vary the length, structure and rhythm of their sentences and to establish cohesion and indicate relationships between and among elements within sentences in sophisticated ways. They often begin their sentences with subjects but have at their disposal other effective strategies for beginning sentences, in the interest, again, of rhythm, variety, and cohesion. They have vocabularies broad enough to select appropriate, concrete, and specific words for a variety of rhetorical contexts. They adhere rigorously to the conventions of Standard English. Strong first-year writers tend to be cautious and conservative in their use of figurative language, occasionally quoting metaphors used by source authors but eschewing figurative language themselves. Their work has that upright, formal tone that their rigorous adherence to the conventions of Standard English engenders, though its probity may be undermined—in a good way—by the use of a first- or second-person point of view, which helps deflect criticism that the style is too remote, unfriendly, pompous, or pretentious.

Knowing these qualities of an effective writing style will help your students revise their own writing to improve its style. But style is the subtlest of the qualities of good writing and, for most freshmen, the ability to recognize a good style when they see it will not translate into the ability to revise their own work to improve its style. Chapter 10 also discusses a variety of instructional strategies including stylistic analysis, sentence combining, and vocabulary building that will help you teach your students how to revise for style. Again, the read-aloud is an excellent strategy for improving style because prose that "sounds good," that "reads well" is prose that has a felicitous style, while prose without that sense of rhythm and flow falls flat when read aloud and will need to be revised.

The 4S revision taxonomy offers a simple mnemonic that will help students remember what they are supposed to do when they revise their work. It may not guarantee that they will apply it successfully and hereafter produce well-organized, robust, sequential, and stylish texts. But if your students know exactly what the components of the revising process are, they will certainly be more ready and willing to revise and, likely, more able, as well.

Chapter Eleven
TEACHING STUDENTS HOW TO EDIT THEIR WRITING

Editing is the process of altering, improving, and correcting punctuation, usage, spelling, grammar, mechanics, and sentence structure in a draft of a written work. It is distinct from its rhetorical cousin revision, which is the process of changing and improving whole paragraphs or the overall structure of a piece of writing, though certainly the editing and revising processes overlap as a writer composes, and distinctions between the two processes blur.

There are, literally, hundreds of editing rules. I set out to count them, one morning, and lost track of time, until, at 2:45, one of my grad students appeared at my office door to ask me if I planned to participate in our seminar that had begun at 2:30. I estimate that there are about three hundred editing rules. There are rules within rules within rules. One basic rule, for example, is that a subject must agree with its verb; within that rule are more rules that govern words intervening between subject and verb, two subjects joined together by "and," two subjects joined together by "or," indefinite pronouns used as subjects, and collective nouns used as subjects. A collective noun will take a singular or a plural verb depending upon whether or not those who make up the collective noun are acting as individuals or together as a group.

There are a dozen rules that govern verb tense, scores that govern pronoun case, reference, and agreement. Writers should be wary of sentence fragments, run-on sentences, misplaced and dangling modifiers, faulty parallelism. There are thirteen or so punctuation marks in English, each of which has its own set of rules; there are fourteen rules that govern the use of the comma alone. And usage—don't get me started: affect and effect, less than and fewer than, different from and different than, which and that, imply and infer, among and between, bring and take, as and like, disinterested and uninterested, regardless and irregardless, can and may. Usage glossaries in composition handbooks typically contain at least a hundred entries.

The story goes from bad to worse. There are exceptions to many of the rules. Sentence fragments are bad unless they are used deliberately, for a particular rhetorical effect—for emphasis, for example—in which case they are good. Commas separate words in a series, except for the word before the "and," unless you are British or Canadian (who spell honor honour and neighbor neighbour) in which case you include that comma. "That" introduces restrictive clauses and "which," nonrestrictive clauses, but "which" can also introduce restrictive clauses.

There are rules even the experts do not agree on. Some of these experts would condemn the previous sentence because it ends in a preposition and would insist the sentence be written: There are rules on which (upon which?) the experts do not agree. Others would argue that the rule about ending a sentence with a preposition is an archaic refugee from the days when Latin was the basis of English grammar. When President Reagan, in his second Inaugural Address, posed the question: "If not us, who?" outraged grammarians fired off letters to newspaper editors, some "experts" claiming "us" should be "we," some claiming "who" should be "whom." Others fired back, purporting to prove why the president's question was, in fact, grammatically correct. Some

61

experts say it's ok to use a plural pronoun to refer back to an indefinite pronoun (Kolln); handbook authors generally insist upon a singular pronoun, though now they want both the masculine and the feminine forms used. The sentence "He or she dove into the pool" is perfectly acceptable in some parts of the country, condemned in other parts by pedants who insist "dived" is the correct past tense form (Lindemann 68).

Professional writers regularly break or ignore the rules. This sentence, for example, appeared in an issue of the *Chicago Tribune*: The cost of hospital AIDS tests vary widely (Burchfield 36). The subject "cost" is singular so the verb should be singular as well: varies, not vary. This sentence appeared in another city newspaper: Each candidate will have ten minutes to present their platform (Soles 30). "Candidate" is clearly singular, so the plural pronoun "their" is not supposed to refer to the singular candidate; "their" should be "his or her." This sentence—There were less people about, as the weather was chilly—is also incorrect: "less" should be changed to "fewer" because "people" are countable (Burchfield 451). "The passive voice should be avoided" one writing textbook recommends in a sentence written in passive voice (Williams). Descriptive grammarians have no problem with these constructions because they believe current usage in published prose determines what is correct. Prescriptive grammarians, who insist writers abide by the accepted and established rules of grammar and usage, go ballistic when they see errors in the work of professional writers, who should be role models to their less literate readers.

Radical teachers, whose influence is growing, don't care much at all for the rules of English grammar and usage. The rules, taken together, form Standard English, or, as it is also known, Edited American English. Some radical teachers resent the academy's insistence on the use of Standard English, arguing that it undemocratic, the code of those with social and political power. Our insistence upon the use of SE perpetuates the vicious power circle and denies or at least inhibits access to power to those students—minorities especially—who were not raised in a culture in which SE was used and valued.

And here is the most disheartening news of all: composition research indicates that teaching the rules of Standard English does not make students better writers. In fact, in his meta-analysis of five studies of the efficacy of grammar instruction, George Hillocks Jr. found that teaching grammar actually had a deleterious effect on writing, probably because such instruction takes time away from more valuable pedagogical activities. The effect size (a measure, expressed as a standard deviation, of the difference between an experimental group and a control group) for grammar instruction was –29, the only instructional strategy of the six Hillocks examined, which had a negative rating. Other studies (see Hartwell and Lindemann 70–73) replicate these findings.

In summary, then, there are too many rules to teach, the rules are rather arbitrary, they perpetuate an imbalance of social power, and teaching them doesn't help anyway. But our students, their parents, administrators, and the general public expect instruction in Standard English to be a part of a writing curriculum. And instruction in Standard English has strong proponents even among those in our profession who know the research. The November 1996 and the January 2003 issues of the *English Journal* addressed the issue of grammar instruction in articles that were largely positive. In book-length studies, Constance Weaver and Rei Noguchi also argue in favor of some grammar instruction, and offer innovative approaches to presenting such instruction, even while they acknowledge the limitations of a component-skills approach to composition instruction.

We are obligated to teach some editing skills in our writing classes. But we cannot expect our students to master three hundred editing rules, so what rules do we teach and how do we teach them?

Three Methods

Most writing teachers take their textbooks as their guide and cover those errors in grammar, sentence structure, punctuation, mechanics, that the text they are using covers. It is almost always necessary to be selective. The latest (2007) edition of the first-year composition text we are currently using at my university has fifty-five chapters, twenty-seven of which are devoted to explanations of editing rules in one form or another. But our instructors devote an average of four classes to instruction and practice in the rules of editing, so obviously not all rules can be taught. Teachers typically choose to teach those editing errors they feel are most important or those that, in their experience, students make most frequently.

Another possibility is to find, in the research, information about editing errors students habitually make and to focus teaching on those errors. Connors and Lunsford examined error patterns in 3,000 student essays and identified the editing errors students make most frequently, as follows:

1. Spelling
2. Missing comma after an introductory element
3. Vague pronoun reference
4. Missing comma in a compound sentence
5. Wrong word
6. Missing comma(s) with a nonrestrictive element
7. Wrong or missing verb ending
8. Wrong or missing preposition
9. Comma splice
10. Missing or misplaced possessive apostrophe
11. Unnecessary shift in tense
12. Unnecessary shift in pronoun
13. Sentence fragment
14. Wrong tense or verb form
15. Lack of agreement between subject and verb
16. Missing comma in a series
17. Lack of agreement between pronoun and antecedent
18. Unnecessary comma(s) with a restrictive element
19. Fused sentence
20. Dangling or misplaced modifier
21. Its/It's confusion.

(in Connors and Glenn 108)

The problem with this plan is that, even though the Connors/Lunsford study does include a wide representative sample, it does not necessarily match the errors your students habitually make. The study was originally published in 1987, when spell checkers were less ubiquitous than they are today, so it is likely spelling errors are no longer first on the list. Colleagues to whom I have shown the list invariably shake their heads and claim the order does not match their own experience. It does not match my own. My own experience tells me sentence fragments and the its/it's confusion should be higher on the list and wrong word and vague pronoun reference should be lower down.

Practical Instruction in Editing Conventions

A third possibility is to provide practical instruction in editing conventions by teaching those editing skills our students are having the most trouble grasping, as revealed in the essays and other writing assignments they do in our classes. To use this strategy, we need to monitor and record the editing errors students in each of our classes are making and tailor our instruction in editing to the real needs of each class. First, we have to make a list consisting of all of the sentences that contain errors our students have written. Then we have to design a taxonomy of editing errors based upon those error-ridden sentences so we can teach students how to recognize and avoid the errors they are making. We can design a series of mini-taxonomies of editing errors after we have graded each assignment and present our practical instruction in editing conventions after we return each assignment. If we have set aside a block of time in our syllabus for instruction in editing conventions, we can gather together all of the faulty sentences which have appeared in assignments we have collected up until the point in the course when we are to teach editing conventions, design our taxonomy, and present the lessons. This is the simpler method and the one I, personally, prefer.

The last time I provided practical instruction in editing conventions in my first-year composition class, I first collected a total of forty-one flawed sentences from writing assignments completed by the tenth week of a fifteen-week class. I divided them, as I usually do, into five categories: errors in sentence grammar, errors in sentence structure, errors in style, errors in punctuation, and errors in diction. I had eight sentences that illustrated common errors in sentence grammar; nine that illustrated common errors in sentence structure; six for style; eleven for punctuation; and seven for diction. The sentences were presented on a worksheet under each of the five categories. Over the course of four fifty-minute classes, we worked our way through the sentences, identifying the errors, learning the rule that applied to the error, and suggesting ways of correcting the errors. Our format was whole-class discussion, though it would certainly be possible to adapt parts of the activity—suggestions for correcting the errors, for example—to a small-group format.

To be sure, there are disadvantages to this particular method of teaching the conventions of Standard English. The most obvious disadvantage is that students might not receive instruction in those important editing conventions for which a sample sentence is not available because students in the class made no errors which illustrated one or more of those editing errors. In my last first-year composition class, for example, we did not cover, among other editing concerns, the dangling modifier, faulty parallelism, faulty subject-verb agreement as it relates to indefinite pronouns acting as subjects, and several of the rules that govern the use of the comma and semicolon, because we had no student-generated sentences to illustrate these concerns.

This method is also labor intensive. The teacher must design a separate taxonomy of error for each writing class he or she teaches, since different students in different classes are going to make different types of errors. Many high school and college writing teachers teach four, even five, sections of composition, and collecting, sorting through, arranging, and writing worksheets or overheads for four or five sets of editing errors will increase an already heavy workload.

But I believe the advantages of such practical instruction in editing conventions outweigh the disadvantages. The great advantage of the method is that, because the examples are drawn from their own work, students are more engaged in learning how to edit effectively. In his study of error patterns in student writing, David Bartholomae concludes that if writing teachers ask students to "share in the process of investigating and interpreting the patterns of error in their writing," students are more likely "to change, experiment, imagine other strategies" (265).

Instruction is also more relevant to students if it revolves around those errors they are actually struggling with in their own writing. By drawing errors from student work and by working through corrections to those errors with their students, writing teachers establish a relevant context within which students can learn. These are not random sentences taken from the end of a chapter in a composition textbook. They are actual sentences students wrote in essays for this class. In his or her book on teacher grammar, Weaver validates the influence of context in the teaching of writing.

One of our goals as writing teachers is to teach students those editing skills they need to master in order to write clearly. Time constraints usually make it impossible to teach all of these skills, but we can teach those that will benefit our students the most if we use the classroom as our laboratory and the student writing as one of the building blocks of our curriculum.

Chapter Twelve
TWO CHEERS FOR PEER RESPONSE

Group work has long been a part of most first-year writing programs, but recent interest in the social construction of knowledge has validated collaborative learning and enshrined group work as a key instructional strategy in the contemporary writing classroom. Most writing teachers now regularly divide students into small groups to brainstorm topics, to discuss the style and content of an essay from the course reader, to create a written text collaboratively, and to critique, constructively, drafts of each other's work. This last activity, variously known as peer response, peer conferencing, or workshopping is especially widespread in first-year composition classes. Not all composition teachers are sold on the efficacy of peer response, but theory and research suggest that, implemented thoughtfully and carefully, it is an effective instructional strategy.

The Case Against Peer Response

Many writing teachers are reluctant to divide their classes into peer response groups, arguing that students neither enjoy the experience, nor do they have the background and experience they need to respond to writing effectively. Indeed, even compositionists who are proponents of peer response groups acknowledge the challenge of facilitating peer response groups that genuinely help students improve their writing.

Some experienced first-year writing teachers are reluctant to divide their students into peer response groups, having witnessed what an uncomfortable experience it is for some students. Passing judgment on another's writing is like passing judgment on another's personal appearance, in that both are expressions and extensions of the self. Many eighteen-year-olds are reticent by nature, especially in a college classroom and have trouble offering advice to classmates about something as personal and high-stakes as a writing assignment. Some have fragile egos and shaky self-esteem and don't take criticism well, even when their peers are trying to be constructive. Others bristle at criticism and their hostility can shut a group down. Students who are products of those cultures that revere the authority of the teacher might mistrust the opinions of their classmates. The dynamics of group interaction are complex, risky, often intense, and some writing teachers feel the benefits are not worth the stress.

Another argument against peer response asserts that students do not really know how to judge each other's writing. Diana George studied peer response groups in first-year writing classes and found that, while some groups are task oriented and do function productively, many do not. Students in what she calls "Leaderless" groups "are very quiet and hesitant about the work they are doing and often look as if they are doing nothing but reading to themselves, not exchanging ideas at all" (321). Students in what she terms "Dysfunctional" groups can barely summon up the effort to put their desks in a circle, seem baffled by their mandate, and can't wait until the whole ordeal is over. Even students in the generally successful "Task Oriented" groups tended to forget the good advice their peers had given them, between the time the group met and the time they sat down to revise their work, in light of the peer response (322).

Thomas Newkirk identifies another peer response pitfall: Students who review a peer's draft and make suggestions for improvement don't necessarily value the same features of a written text that the teacher, who will be grading the text, values. Newkirk asked ten writing teachers and ten students to respond to four student essays. The two groups agreed on the merit of two of the essays but disagreed on two others, and on one of those the disagreement was enormous. Students gave an essay about friendship an average score, on a ten-point scale, of 6.7, while teachers gave the same essay an average score of 3.9. Imagine the author of the friendship essay, satisfied by the response of his or her peers, confidently turning his or her paper in to his or her teacher, only to be crushed and confused when he or she gets back a paper with a low grade.

Brooke, Mirtz, and Evans identify three stumbling blocks to effective group work. Usually group members are not friends or family members and so it is necessary to establish a level of trust within the group if peer response is to be honest. Writing is often personal and it takes time and effort to foster the trust necessary for a group to work well. The second stumbling block is that a group may not gel because the group members might be so diverse in age, race, and life experience that they have trouble working well together. Finally, teachers simply cannot devote to group work the class time that is necessary for group member to work together productively and harmoniously.

In her comprehensive study of peer response groups, Karen Spears notes that groups often flounder because students are confused about the group's purpose and their roles in it; they cannot read each other's texts analytically; they don't understand the nature of the writing process, the role of revision, especially; they do not know how to work collaboratively; and they cannot self-monitor and keep momentum within the group going (17–18). They tend, therefore, to take an easy way out, going through the motions but hoping "to keep discussion safe, objective, and non-threatening" (24). They focus on helping each other produce a text that is correct rather than interesting and insightful because they believe their teachers value most writing free from errors in grammar, spelling, and punctuation.

Effective Peer Response

Despite her thorough analysis of the drawbacks of peer response, Spears is a strong advocate of peer response pedagogy. In *Sharing Writing*, she presents a comprehensive guide for writing teachers who want to use peer response successfully as the nexus of their curriculum. She includes a transcript of an effective peer response session and annotates the transcript, explaining the sub-text of students' conversation and detailing the reasons why this session is successful. She patiently explains how to start a peer-centered writing class, using her own experiences, both positive and negative, as the model and explains, as well, the nature of the change in mindset—on the parts of both teacher and students—essential for successful peer conferencing. She includes a chapter on teaching students how to read each other's work actively and analytically. She includes a chapter on helping students cultivate the continuum of listening skills they need—attending, reflecting, drawing out, and connecting (123)—if they are to respond effectively to a fellow student's draft. Referencing cybernetics, she includes a chapter on giving effective supportive and editorial feedback and on delaying challenging feedback until "the group has established secure working relations and has learned some preliminary analytical skills and how to convey responses effectively" (134).

Spears certainly convinces readers her approach to teaching writing is effective. She believes in the social constructionist theory behind peer response, and she clearly succeeds in transforming theory into practice. Many writing teachers, however, will be reluctant to commit themselves so totally to one pedagogy, to teach the reading, listening, and group dynamic skills Spears and her followers teach to ensure the success of their method. Still, they want their students to reap the benefits of group work. Fortunately, we can provide our students with the benefits of peer response without sacrificing other instructional strategies that work well for us. But even if we devote as little as a half an hour a week of class time to peer response, we still need to adhere to the guidelines that make peer response effective.

First, we must <u>train</u> our students how to work in peer response groups productively and effectively. At a minimum, we need a mini-lesson, supplemented perhaps by a videotape on effective collaboration, to teach our students that there are some behaviors that will promote the success of group work and others that will anticipate its failure. Readers must be clear and direct in their assessment of their classmates' work, but discrete and respectful in the way they offer suggestions for improvement, proffering praise as well as blame throughout the process. Writers must leave their hostility at the door and be open and receptive to their peers' suggestions, even if, after honest reflection, they choose not to make a change a peer has proposed. If we choose to devote more time to training, the class can observe each group in action, then learn from listening to the teacher's assessment of how and why members of each group worked productively and/or not so productively together.

Wei Zhu compared the peer response protocols of an experimental group of first-year composition students trained in effective peer response strategies with those of a control group who received only superficial training. The results of her study indicate that students who were trained gave more feedback and more substantive feedback to each other and were more enthusiastic about the peer response process.

Nancy Grimm also advocates training to facilitate effective peer response. She trains her students by providing them with and discussing a set of written "Guidelines for Writing Groups" (91). In the guidelines, Grimm specifies the amount of time students will have to peer conference, presents ways of helping writers overcome any sensitivity they might have about sharing their work, shows how peers can respond in ways that will encourage helpful revision, without undermining their classmates' self confidence, and describes ways of keeping students on task. She also recommends teachers model for their students appropriate and effective behavior and participation by joining each group as a participant on a regular basis. With the teacher's guidance, the students can ask "the hard questions that ask the writer to re-think his subject, forcing him back to the chaos of an early draft but eventually bringing a sharper focus and more thorough development" (93).

Second, we must <u>limit the scope</u> of a peer response session. If we organize students into groups and simply instruct them to read and respond to drafts of each other's essays, we doom the session to failure. Students will flounder, focus on surface-level errors, and soon drift into a discussion about who the winner of the latest reality show will be. If we ask groups to achieve one or two specific goals—consider the appeal of each other's thesis, the development of the paragraphs in the body of the paper, the precision of the diction the writer uses—students will stay on task, their discussion will be more pointed, and they increase the chances that the quality of their work will improve. Lindemann recommends limiting peer response to thirty minutes, at most, and giving the groups specific work, defined concretely (206).

Third, we must provide students with specific criteria upon which to evaluate each other's work. If, for example, the session is on the efficacy of the opening of their persuasive essays, students should have a checklist that presents characteristics of an effective opening for a persuasive essay, and they should evaluate each other's work in the context of that checklist. Open-ended conversation starters also work well, especially if your students are prone to checking off the criteria on a rubric perfunctorily. According to Lindemann, a good conversation starter from a writer's perspective is "The main point I wanted to get across in this paragraph was. . ." (206), while a good starter from the reader's perspective is "As a reader, the part of your paper that most confused me was. . ." (206).

Finally, we must monitor the progress of each group during the peer response session. It is tempting to use the time to grade; we may be reluctant to eavesdrop; but it is crucial to keep students on task, especially freshmen, prone to drifting off topic. Diana George insists teachers must circulate, listen, and look for opportunities to join groups to keep discussion focused (325). Lindemann counsels teachers to make a "quick pass through the class in the first few minutes of an activity to be sure all students understand what they are supposed to do" (207). Thereafter, the teacher should discretely observe one group at a time but should respond to group requests for the teacher's opinion with "a question that helps the group examine the draft more closely or enables the students to arbitrate the issue themselves" (207) since an important goal of peer response is to help students learn how to revise their writing independently. Lindemann also suggests teachers take some time at the end of a peer response session to debrief, especially to share with students reasons why one or more of the groups functioned successfully.

Co-Authoring

A slightly different but equally effective take on small-group work is the in-class, co-authored writing assignment. Instead, for example, of giving students forty minutes of class time to read and constructively criticize each other's opening paragraphs to a persuasive essay, consider having the group compose such a paragraph together.

Co-authoring does not work especially well if students bring a prepared assignment with them to class to mix together with other prepared assignments to produce one excellent text. Students will tend to select what they consider to be the best work, suggest minor changes, submit it, and call it a day. And it is true that, as with peer editing, the strong personalities in the group will contribute the most to the developing text.

But there are benefits to in-class, co-authored assignments. Indeed, such assignments provide most of the benefits and avoid some of the drawbacks of peer response. The downside of peer response is, of course, self-consciousness. Many students are shy about sharing their work with others. A co-authoring exercise may not eliminate but will reduce this anxiety. Students are not putting on display work they have already done; they are contributing, with their peers, to a work in progress. Moreover, a co-authoring exercise is even more active and constructive an activity than peer conferencing, in that students are building a text together, not simply making suggestions for a text already in draft form. In co-authoring sessions, students do learn from others rhetorical strategies they can then apply to the work they do alone (Dale). Students enjoy co-authoring more than they do peer editing (Shepherd-Wynn). And this form of collaboration helps prepare students for those careers which depend upon the ability to work with others on various projects, most of which require writing.

Whether the group is composing a text together or editing each other's texts, group work does not lighten a writing teacher's workload, but may, in fact, increase it if we factor into the mix the time and effort it takes to convince apathetic students of its value. But implemented carefully, even if sparingly, it does have value. Group work helps prepare students for work in corporate America, where many projects require a collaborative effort. It sharpens active reading and listening and critical thinking skills. And it reminds students that writing must have a purpose that real live readers can discern.

Chapter Thirteen

HELPING STUDENTS CULTIVATE AN EFFECTIVE WRITING STYLE

As first-year writing teachers, we strive to help students generate writing that is intelligent and informative, clear and substantial. We also want our students to learn to write with a little flair and energy, to cultivate an effective writing style. Government reports may be informative and substantial, but they tend, as well, to be prosaic, to reflect the nature of the bureaucrats who write them and the gray confines within which they work. We work to encourage our students to put some color into their writing, to eschew the monotonic style of so much government and corporate communication. The purpose of this chapter is to present a detailed analysis of the style of exemplary first-year writing in order to establish and understand those features of written discourse that first-year writing teachers most value and reward. Having established the features of the style of exemplary first-year writing, the chapter goes on to provide first-year composition teachers with some suggestions that can help them help their students cultivate an excellent writing style.

To accomplish these goals, we need examples of exemplary first-year writing and a matrix that analyses the style of written discourse. As examples of exemplary first-year writing, we use three model first-year research papers, taken from three current, widely used first-year composition handbooks. The authors of these books have selected examples of excellent student essays to include in their texts as models for other students to study and emulate, as they work their own way through the writing process. Style, of course, is mediated by rhetorical mode: a personal narrative has a casual style, an email to a friend, an intimate style; a government report, an impersonal style. Our models are researched academic essays, a mode which presupposes a relatively conservative, a "Standard English" style, privileged within the academy.

Three Exemplary Essays

In *Universal Keys for Writers*, Ann Raimes includes a model student essay, "Hollywood and Historical Accuracy," by Jacob Radford (828–836). Radford's thesis is that many movies that claim to be historically accurate are really not; that producers, for commercial reasons, often alter history to make the story they are telling more entertaining and appealing. He cites many examples but focuses his essay on a study of the historical accuracy of director Milos Forman's film *Amadeus*, an adaptation of Peter Shaffer's dramatic biography of Mozart. Radford echoes the concerns of some historians, whom he cites, who worry that students are getting a distorted view of important historical events, such as the assassination of President Kennedy, because they are accepting fictionalized film versions of such events as the absolute truth. Radford cites fourteen sources to support his thesis.

In the fourth edition of *The Blair Handbook*, Toby Fulwiler and Alan Hayakawa include a model student paper "The Two Freedoms of Henry David Thoreau" by Andrew Turner (785–793). Turner's thesis is that Thoreau, in "On the Duty of Civil Disobedience" and *Walden: Or, Life in the Woods*, redefined the concept of individual freedom. In "On the Duty of Civil Disobedience," Thoreau makes the case against any government intervention in the life of the individual. In *Walden*, Thoreau proves how an individual can also be free from society's demands, constraints, and expectations by living a simple and completely self-sufficient life. Turner discusses the influence Thoreau's work had on influential social and political leaders like Gandhi and Martin Luther King Jr. To support his argument, he cites six sources in addition to the two works by Thoreau.

In the sixth edition of *The Bedford Handbook*, Diana Hacker includes a model student essay, "A Call to Action: Regulate Use of Cell Phones on the Road," by Angela Daly (637–645). Daly's thesis is that it is dangerous to drive and talk on a cell phone at the same time and that laws need to be established to prohibit this dangerous practice. Daly supports her thesis with an impressive array of facts and figures that prove what a menace drivers who talk on their cell phones can be. She discusses fatal traffic accidents caused, in large part, by drivers who were distracted because they were talking on their phones. She cites scientific studies, including one from *The New England Journal of Medicine*, which confirm the dangers of dialing and talking while driving. She criticizes politicians for failing to pass laws curtailing the use of cell phones and disparages the few laws that do exist because they don't punish offenders to the extent needed. She praises countries like Japan that have established laws prohibiting drivers from using cell phones and notes the dramatic reduction in cell-phone related accidents after such laws were passed. Daly cites eleven sources in support of her thesis.

Style Analysis

Having found our examples of exemplary first-year writing, we need, of course, a matrix or a taxonomy that will help us analyze and describe the style of these essays. For this, we turn to Edward P.J. Corbett, arguably our profession's leading expert in the analysis of writing styles, specifically to his book *Classical Rhetoric for the Modern Student*. Corbett has a thorough and detailed matrix, a prose style chart, for analyzing a writer's style (415–423). It is a system based on the application of mathematical computations to rhetorical features to establish a numerically based stylistic analysis. Indeed, Corbett measures almost fifty different indices that establish the nature of a writer's style. He computes average sentence and paragraph length; he examines the grammatical types of sentences and the rhetorical elements with which sentences begin; he measures the number of monosyllabic words a writer uses against the number of multi-syllabic words; he calculates the number of and assesses the nature of the nouns, verbs, and adjectives a written text contains.

An analysis of the results of the application of Corbett's matrix to our three examples of excellent first-year writing reveals much about the writing style that experienced first-year writing teachers (and textbook authors) value in the work of their students. We learn, for example, that the average length of an exemplary first-year essay, at least one that requires research and the citing of sources, is 1,395 words, divided into 62 sentences. (Corbett's matrix does not compute average number of paragraphs but that number is 10.6, so the average paragraph length in words is

131.6). The average length of a sentence in an excellent first-year paper is 22.5 words, about the same as that for experienced adult writers (Hunt). The average paragraph contains 5.6 sentences.

More interesting and revealing are the grammatical types of sentences valued in first-year writing. Indices of syntactic maturity indicate that better, more experienced writers use subordinate conjunctions and relative pronouns to combine sentences together, while less experienced writers tend to rely more heavily on coordinate conjunctions (Loban; O'Hare). In the exemplary writing of college freshmen, then, we would expect to see much more subordination than coordination, and this is precisely what the application of Corbett's matrix to our excellent freshmen writers reveals. An average of 38.3 percent of the sentences in our model compositions are complex; another 9.3 percent are compound-complex, for a total of 47.6 percent of sentences that use subordination to combine clauses. Only, on average, 9.6 percent of the sentences are compound sentences, those joined together with a coordinate conjunction. An average of 41 percent of the sentences in the study are simple, but the use of the simple sentences does not indicate syntactic immaturity because a sentence may be reduced to a phrase, even to a word and be combined with a main clause to create a simple sentence. It is the frequent joining together of simple sentences with coordinate conjunctions that mark an immature writing style, and this is why comparatively few sentences in the essays examined here are compound.

Variety in syntactical choices for sentence openers is another marker of a sophisticated style. Sentences typically begin with a subject, of course, and in most mature written texts half of the sentences are likely to begin with a subject. But to achieve some sentence variety and to vary and enhance the rhythm and flow of the prose, good writers tend to vary the subject as sentence opener with other syntactical elements: a phrase, a clause, or a word other than a noun or pronoun. An average of 45.3 percent of the sentences in our models of exemplary first-year writing opened with a subject. The percent averages for other sentence openers, in descending order of frequency are:

Prepositional phrase:	20.3
Single adverb:	11.6
Adverb clause:	7.3
Verbal phrase:	5.6
Expletive:	3.0
Coordinate conjunction:	2.6
Conjunctive phrase:	2.6
Absolute phrase:	1.0
Front shift:	0.3
Adjective phrase:	0.0

Finally, Corbett's prose style chart assesses a writer's word choice or diction. Note that the analysis here does not include the whole text but is limited to several paragraphs, since, to examine word choice in the whole text of a thousand-plus-word essay, even with the assistance of a computer, would be very time consuming. Here, we conduct a diction analysis of paragraphs three, four, and five of the Radford and Daly essays, and, to assure a comparable word count, of paragraphs three, four, five, and six of the Turner essay.

We would expect excellent first-year writers to have a vocabulary ample enough that they can access the most accurate word for the rhetorical context within which they are working. Corbett's matrix measures monosyllabic substantive words against multi-syllabic words on the grounds that an ability to call up a multi-syllabic word suggests syntactic maturity. These grounds are shaky: the monosyllabic word might be the most effective in a given rhetorical context. But a high percentage of monosyllabic words likely does suggest a limited vocabulary and, hence, a simpler style. It should not be surprising, then, that an average of just 19.6 percent of the substantive words in our three examples of excellent first-year writing are monosyllabic.

When teaching effective diction, composition teachers and textbooks generally recommend the use of concrete and specific nouns rather than vague and abstract nouns, because the concrete word sharpens meaning and helps orient a reader's senses (Fulwiler and Hayakawa 390; Hacker 230-31; Raimes 620). We see a "big Mercedes" clearer than we see a "big car," a college first-year student "absorbed by *An Introduction to Quantum Mechanics*" clearer than one "reading a textbook." Not surprisingly, good first-year writers use more concrete than abstract nouns: an average of 65.3 percent of the nouns and pronouns in the passages from our three model essays are concrete.

Similarly, we advise our students to limit the use of linking verbs, which are less precise than regular or irregular verbs, and which can impair concision, and writing teachers generally see concision as another marker of an effective style (Fulwiler and Hayakawa 392). "He or she danced beautifully on opening night" is better writing than "He or she was a beautiful dancer on opening night." Stylistically, a sentence like "Fitzgerald's colorful and ornate style reflects perfectly the Jazz-Age-setting setting of his novels" is better than "Fitzgerald's colorful and ornate style is a perfect reflection of the Jazz-Age-setting of his novels." It is not surprising, then, that an average of a mere 1.7 percent of the words in the passages analyzed are liking verbs.

Like linking verbs, verbs in passive voice are usually considered less efficient than active-voice verbs, and most writing handbooks advise against their overuse (Fulwiler and Hayakawa 396; Hacker 136; Raimes 419). The passive is fine when an active subject is indeterminate: "Smoking is forbidden." But the passive is wordy when a natural subject is in the sentence. Clearly a sentence like "A great novel was written by Fitzgerald" is more stylistically cumbersome than "Fitzgerald wrote a great novel." Only an average of 1.3 percent of the words in the passages from our three model essays are passive-voice verbs.

The felicitous use of figurative language is another marker of a writer's style. Corbett's matrix does not account for figurative language, but he discusses it thoroughly in his book (424–460), defining and giving examples of every figure of speech the language accommodates. He advises student writers to "make a conscious effort to use figures when you see that they will suit your purpose" (*Classical* 458). Devet bemoans the diminishing emphasis writing teachers place on the use of figurative language and argues that modern views of language and approaches to the teaching of writing support additional instruction in the use of not just metaphor but of sophisticated figures of speech such as anaphora, epistrophe, anadiplosis, polysyndeton, asyndeton, and antimetabole. Peterson agrees, asserting that metaphor enriches student writing and offering strategies to help students learn to use metaphors effectively. Raimes, in contrast, advises student writers to "Use figurative language for effect, but use it sparingly" (625). Fulwiler and Hayakawa, similarly, advise their readers to use figurative language, "not for ornament or embellishment, but to help readers understand your meaning" (449); and Hacker also counsels restraint, advising writers to "use figures of speech with care" (237). Used carelessly, figurative language can become mixed metaphors and clichés, which mark a weak writing style.

Judging from our three examples, figurative language is, indeed, used sparingly in excellent first-year essays. Raimes' student discusses films which "run the gamut of accuracy" (828) and cautions that "No one should expect gospel truth on the silver screen" (833). Fulwiler and Hayakawa's student quotes Thoreau's expressed wish to "take rank hold on life and spend [his] day more as animals do" (790), but he uses no figurative language of his own. Hacker's student quotes a spokesperson from a cell phone company, who is worried about a "crazy patchwork quilt of ordinances" (642) regulating cell phone use and a legislator who claims the issue of regulating cell phone use while driving is "gaining steam around the country" (643). But he or she uses just one metaphor of his or her own, comparing cell-phone-using motorists to "drunk drivers, weaving between lanes" (637). Apparently, the best student writers use figurative language sparingly and tend not to generate or select original figurative language when they use it themselves or quote the figurative language of others.

Another important quality of style in written discourse is voice or tone, the personality and attitude a writer projects through word choice, sentence length and variety, rhetorical mode, and point of view. Corbett's prose style chart does not consider voice, probably because it is not measurable in the same way sentence length and structure is. Hacker advises that a "chatty, breezy voice is usually not welcome in a research paper, but neither is a stuffy, pretentious style or a timid, unsure one" (574). Fulwiler and Hayakawa, similarly, recommend an "authoritative voice," one that is "clear, direct, factual, and specific, leaving the impression that the writer is confident about what he or she is saying" (71). Walker Gibson suggests there are essentially three voices—tough, sweet, stuffy—within which modern American writers work.

An analysis of our three exemplary student essays suggests that some range in voice is acceptable in the academic writing of college freshmen. Naturally, all essays adhere to the dictates of Standard English; their level of vocabulary and sentence structure is comparatively sophisticated; and they are well researched. As a result, their voice is appropriately academic: neither pompous and pedantic nor chatty and breezy. It is conservative, cautious, and remote. But there are differences in point of view among the three essays, and point of view exerts considerable influence on voice.

Raimes' student uses a neutral, objective, third-person point of view throughout most of his essay, but shifts, in one sentence in his eighth paragraph, to second person. He is making the point that filmmakers embellish reality to make their stories more interesting. Then he abruptly jumps out of third person and into second when he addresses his readers personally: "If *you* [italics mine] were to tell your life story, would you tell the exact truth—would you even be able to recall an exact truth—or would you embellish some areas, even just a little" (831). He returns to his objective point of view, then, in his twelfth paragraph, he inserts a sentence in first-person point of view. He is making the point that a movie about a historical event, even one that is not historically accurate, can stimulate interest in the subject: "If I found a story interesting," Radford writes, "I would probably do research on the material, as I am doing with Mozart right now" (833). The shifts are jarring, moving as they do from academic/persuasive to narrative and from distant to familiar, though that more familiar tone they create is not necessarily inappropriate in the writing of a freshman.

Hacker's student uses first-person plural point of view in his or her essay, which begins "When a cell phone goes off in a classroom or at a concert, *we* [italics mine] are irritated but at least our lives are not endangered" (637). Fulwiler and Hayakawa's student consistently uses third person in his essay. His is the conventional, relatively formal voice of the young academic writing a freshman-composition research paper, but, as the tone of the other essays suggests, writing teachers are quite willing to accept the more familiar voice conveyed by a first and a second-person points of view.

In summary, then, the results of our analysis of the style of three exemplary first-year essays suggest that there is an identifiable writing style valued by first-year composition teachers. Excellent first-year writers use subordination effectively to vary the length, structure, and rhythm of their sentences and to establish cohesion and indicate relationships between and among elements within sentences in sophisticated ways. They often begin their sentences with subjects but have at their disposal other effective strategies for beginning sentences, in the interest, again, of rhythm, variety, and cohesion. They have vocabularies broad enough to select appropriate, concrete, and specific words for a variety of rhetorical contexts. They adhere rigorously to the conventions of Standard English. Excellent first-year writers tend to be cautious and conservative in their use of figurative language, occasionally quoting metaphors used by source authors but eschewing figurative language themselves. Their work has that upright, formal tone that their rigorous adherence to the conventions of Standard English engenders, though its probity may be undermined—in a good way—by the use of a first- or second-person point of view, which helps deflect criticism that the style is too remote, unfriendly, pompous, or pretentious.

Cultivating an Effective Writing Style

How can we help our students cultivate a writing style that is effective for an academic essay? We might begin by convincing students that style is an important, identifiable, even measurable, feature of written discourse, one of the five aspects of Aristotelian rhetoric. Here a discussion, with students, of the work of Donald Foster can prove valuable. Foster claims that style is a literary fingerprint, as distinct almost as a literal one, and that he can determine authorship by examining certain stylistic features of a writer's work, the way and the order in which they use words, for example, or the way they punctuate sentences. Using his system, he attributed the anonymously published novel *Primary Colors* to Joe Klein and eventually forced Klein, who had vehemently denied being its author, to fess up. He has worked with law enforcement agencies, providing them with clues for several important cases. He helped police consider the authorship of the ransom note in the JonBenet Ramsey case and of the mysterious writings that turned out to be the work of Unabomber Ted Kaczynski. Foster's work is controversial, and he has had to retract certain claims about authorship he had previously made, notably the authorship of an anonymous poem he had once attributed to Shakespeare. But sharing and discussing Foster's work with students, at a time when several top-rated TV programs are about the importance of forensic science in criminal investigations, can heighten their understanding of style and their awareness of its rhetorical significance.

Winston Weathers also recommends that we motivate students to develop a good style by explaining to them that writers express their individuality through their style. He argues, even, that our freedom to write in a distinct style is a symbol of our political freedom, as well, "a gesture of personal freedom against inflexible states of mind" (369), endemic to less democratic societies. He goes on to outline a pedagogy for teaching style, one that stresses writing original sentences and paragraphs, then re-writing them in a variety of different styles: militant, judicious, elegant, plain, colloquial, formal (372). Finally, he recommends teachers teach style by analyzing the style of their own writing, as they compose brief texts spontaneously in class and share, with students, examples of their own published writing.

Other compositionists also recommend exercises that force students to focus their attention on their own and others' writing styles. Corbett suggests we have our students analyze the style of writing they would do well to emulate, using specific systems of stylistic analysis. He has his students apply his own prose style chart to their writing and to exemplary writing and to consider similarities and differences between the two (Corbett, *Classical*). He provides testimonials from students who found the exercise interesting and helpful in cultivating a better style. He also recommends ("Approaches" 94) students study Flesch's "readability formula," not necessarily to apply it to their own writing, since it champions the use of shorter words and sentences, but "as an easy entrée into stylistic study" (95). Students might also benefit from applying to their own writing Lanham's "paramedic method" of measuring the "lard factor" in a written text and reconsidering aspects of their style in light of Lanham's advice. Kate Ronald urges students to usurp the teachers' role and respond, in writing, to their own writing (207), as a way of heightening their awareness of the strengths and weaknesses of their own style.

Having convinced students that style is an important feature of written discourse, we can turn our attention to helping students improve upon those features of exemplary first-year writing that the study reported here reveals. The number of complex sentences and simple sentences with embedded phrases that we see in exemplary first-year writers urges us to (re)consider sentence-combining training, as a viable instructional strategy. Influential studies conducted in the 1970s illustrated the benefits of sentence combining training (O'Hare; Daiker, Kerek, and Morenberg) and convinced many English teachers to include practice in sentence combining in their composition courses. The sentence-combining star faded when later research suggested that, while sentence combining does improve syntactic maturity, it did not necessarily improve overall writing quality (Faigley; Crowhurst), and it could increase the rate of error in sentence structure, the placement of modifiers, especially. But syntactic maturity is an essential aspect of an effective style and, as such, is a worthy goal for a writing class. Used judiciously, and recognizing their limitations, exercises in sentence combining are a good way of improving students' writing style.

So, too, might practice in writing cumulative sentences, an instructional strategy Francis Christensen advocates. Expert writers, Christensen notes, write "cumulative sentences," ones that have a base clause onto which modifying words, phrases, and clauses have been added. Writing teachers, he recommends, should expose students to well-written cumulative sentences, then provide them with a basic sentence, which they are to expand, based upon the pattern of the model. When they can do this well, they are ready to compose their own cumulative sentences but ones still based upon the pattern and syntax of the model. This exercise, Christensen argues, develop style while reinforcing the importance of elaborating ideas.

Walpole also recommends sentence play as an ally in "the vigorous pursuit of style and grace." She has her students study a model sentence and then re-work and revise it in many ways: changing its diction; deleting, transposing, and transforming certain elements within it; reversing the sentence-combining process by reducing it to a series of short sentences; and finally generating new sentences imitating the pattern of the model. This exercise, she hopes, will "increase our students' sensitivity to words and rhythms . . . enlarge their repertoires of grammatical and stylistic options . . . enhance their appreciation of subtle grace, apt style, clean vigor" (169).

Corbett also champions imitation as an effective exercise to improve students' sentence structure. He presents the testimony of good writers from Malcolm X to Somerset Maugham, in support of his view that neophyte writers who imitate the style of accomplished writers will gradually develop their own unique and effective style. He suggests students begin by copying exemplary passages from the work of famous writers word for word, before they move on to create their own sentences, imitating the pattern, hence the style, of model sentences written, again, by accomplished writers. This exercise, Corbett claims, will pay "high dividends to those who use it conscientiously" (*Classical*, 495), though most writing teachers are going to need more convincing before they assign any word-for-word copying in a composition class, no matter how compelling the style of the copied work might be.

Writing teachers also need to help students build a strong vocabulary if we are to help students cultivate a good style. Corbett implores students to read actively, looking up unfamiliar words in a dictionary and reflecting upon their meaning, especially within the context of the passage they are reading (*Classical*, 385). There is some value, he acknowledges, in simply studying and looking up unfamiliar words on a list a teacher presents to students, but he stresses the advantages of learning unfamiliar words in the context of a passage in which they appear (386). Glenn, Goldthwaite, and Connors also champion avid and active reading, overstating their case, perhaps, when they claim that "[O]nly avid and accomplished readers can generate and perceive style, recognizing it in a contextual continuum" (255).

They are correct, though, in their assertion that stylish prose sounds good. If the structure of the sentences is varied, if the words and phrases are ordered effectively, if the diction is precise and accurate, the prose flows; it has cadence and rhythm. Walpole recommends writing teachers read excellent prose aloud to their students, "just to let students attune their ears to the rhythm and resonance of vigorous prose" (164). Corbett encourages students to read their own work aloud before handing it in to help them create euphonious sentences, specifically "to catch awkward rhythms, clashing vowel and consonant combinations. . . , and distracting jingles" (*Classical*, 408). Ronald, similarly, urges students to read their work aloud to a real person, listening to determine if their work sounds natural or if it sounds like the work of "a student performing for a grade" (205).

We can teach our first-year composition students how to write with style. The ability to write academic discourse with style is not, as some scholars (see Milic) and even some professors assert, an innate gift. It is probably true that gifted poets, novelists, and playwrights are born and not made, that they do have an innate genius for language, a natural facility for using words in a strikingly original, creative, fluid, and rhythmic manner. But academic discourse is more prescribed than creative writing, requiring as it does syntactic maturity, a rich vocabulary, a steady voice, and a commitment to Standard English, all of which are fostered by a teacher's dedication and a student's diligence but none of which presupposes genius.

Chapter Fourteen
SHARING SCORING GUIDES

A scoring guide, also called a criteria scale, a feedback sheet, or a rubric, is a descriptive list of the criteria which teachers use to judge the quality of their students' written work. Analytic or criterion-referenced guides consist of a list of specific aspects of writing performance, often subdivided under main categories such as content, development, grammar, structure, and style. Student essays are graded based on the degree to which the essays match the criteria listed. Teachers typically deduct marks when an essay fails to meet a criterion. Holistic or norm-referenced scoring guides typically consist of a set of paragraphs, which describe the general qualities of outstanding, excellent, good, average, fair, and poor writing for a given assignment. Each paragraph on the holistic scale is numbered, the highest number corresponding to the paragraph that describes the attributes of an outstanding essay, the lowest describing the attributes of a poor essay. A student's essay is graded with the number of the paragraph that most closely describes the attributes of that essay. Composition theory and research indicate that, whether they use a holistic or an analytic rubric, teachers should share their scoring guides with their students. Both students and teachers benefit in many substantial ways when students draft and revise their written work in the context of the rubric their teachers will use to assess student writing.

Students benefit primarily because they will write better essays if they understand the criteria their teachers will use to evaluate their writing. Research suggests a positive correlation between a student's knowledge of evaluative criteria and the grade the student gets on an essay to which that evaluative criteria is applied. Hillocks reviewed eleven studies done between 1963 and 1982 on the use of criteria scales and feedback sheets to improve student writing (156–160). Participants in the studies ranged in level from sixth grade to first-year college. In these studies, an experimental group was given a list of the criteria upon which a particular writing assignment would be judged; a control group was not. In most cases, teachers discussed the criteria with their students and encouraged them to comply with the criteria as they worked on their writing assignments. "Most of the studies involved found statistically significant differences between students using the sets of criteria and those taught through some other technique" (56). After reviewing the studies, Hillocks selected the best six, combined their results and evaluated these results statistically, using a sophisticated technique called a meta-analysis. He reports a mean effect size (a measure of overall difference in performance between experimental and control groups in all six studies combined) of a respectable .36. This rating makes the use of shared scoring guides the second most effective instructional strategy Hillocks investigated, second only to inquiry and ahead of sentence combining, model analysis, free writing, and grammar instruction.

In a well-designed study, Lamm investigated the efficacy of three instructional methods for teaching argumentative writing to college freshmen:

- the study of exemplary models of writing,
- the use of criteria scales, and

- revision which, in this study, involved using a criteria scale to revise a writing sample, which was not written by the students doing the revision exercise.

Two teachers used each of the three treatments in separate writing classes; in other words, six writing classes, a total of 102 students, participated in the study. Results of the study indicate that criteria scales are the most effective of the three methods studied for teaching writing. The effect size for models was 0.19; for revision, 0.48, and for scales 0.54. One instructor's Scales students registered a huge effect size, in excess of a full standard deviation (1.095). Lamm speculates that scales "may offer a better bridge [than models] from declarative to procedural knowledge" (6). In other words, the study of exemplary models of writing teach students <u>what</u> is effective and ineffective (declarative knowledge) but not <u>how</u> to make their own writing more effective (procedural knowledge). Scales do both. Lamm's study also indicates that female students benefit more from the application of scales to their writing than male students do. He also believes scales work especially well for argumentative writing, which makes more intellectual demands on students than other rhetorical modes do.

Wyngaard and Gehrke also experimented with the use of criteria scales to improve student writing. They used a type of analytic rubric, known as a primary trait scale, which focused on three aspects of effective writing: openings, focus, and "showing not telling." They described the qualities of excellent, good, adequate, and ineffective writing across each trait. They discussed the rubrics with their students and gave students written descriptions of the rubrics to help them assess their own work. Finally, they used the rubrics themselves to assess the students' writing. Their study indicates that the use of rubrics is an effective way to improve student writing.

Stoddard and MacArthur found that shared scoring guides improved the narrative writing of learning-disabled students. The seventh- and eighth-grade students who participated in their study worked in pairs to assist each other in revising their writing. The rubric, which they used, prompted the students to examine and critique the parts, order, details, and clarity of each other's narratives (85). As the rubric indicates, the researchers were interested more in substantive rather than mechanical improvement to the students' writing. Students were thoroughly and carefully trained in using the rubrics effectively. Over the course of the study, student writing improved significantly, confirming the efficacy of the use of the rubric. "Improvement for individual students from baseline to posttest ranged from 2.6 to 5.5 points on an eight-point scale" (91).

Research also suggests that shared scoring guides facilitate peer conferencing and render it more effective than it is when students do not work with rubrics. In his or her summary of this research, Zhu (492-96) illustrates how peer conferencing appears to be most effective when students have clear criteria they can use to constructively criticize each other's writing. "Overall, successful peer response groups are task oriented, focus on the global features of writing, provide accurate and specific feedback for one another, and engage in negotiation" (496).

Zhu's own study of peer response groups compared a control group of students which received minimal training in peer response with an experimental group which was well-trained by composition instructors to respond effectively to peer writing. These instructors:

made it clear that, when critiquing peer writing, peers should focus more on global concerns such as development of ideas, audience, purpose, and organization. Often, the teachers explicitly asked students to comment first on aspects related to the content and organization of the essay under discussion. When some students failed to do this and instead first commented on more local features such as grammar, language usage, and word choice, the teacher would briefly discuss students' feedback but would then, using directives, guide students' attention back to the global concerns. . . . (502)

Instructors, in other words, helped students in the experimental group develop specific criteria which they could use to assess the writing of their peers. These experimental-group students were more effective peer evaluators than were their control group counterparts. "The experimental group provided significantly more feedback, significantly more feedback on global features of writing, and significantly more specific and relevant feedback" (509).

Research also suggests that shared scoring guides improve student performance on subsequent writing assignments. Teachers often complain that they painstakingly evaluate their students' writing, carefully making written comments and suggestions for improvement in the margins and at the end of the paper, only to see the same errors and lapses in style recur in subsequent assignments. A study by Clifford (in Hillocks) suggests that students who work with criteria scales transfer to subsequent assignments the skills in revising and editing which the scales fostered. Reviewing this study, Hillocks concludes that "the active application of criteria and subsequent suggestions for improvement in their own and others' writing enabled the students to internalize criteria which then served as guides for their own independent writing" (158). The Stoddard/MacArthur study, discussed above, corroborates this finding. Stoddard and MacArthur speculate that students internalize the rubrics because they continued to write narratives of higher quality after working in peer conferencing sessions with criteria scales.

Shared scoring guides might reduce writing apprehension. Smith (in Hillocks 49–51) reviews research which indicates that students who are apprehensive about writing write less capably than those who have no or only slight apprehension about writing. Their compositions tend to be shorter and they use "significantly less intense language" (50) than students who are not apprehensive about writing. Their grades tend to be lower across the curriculum, and they tend to avoid majors which require a lot of writing. There is no research evidence to suggest apprehension would diminish if apprehensive students knew the criteria upon which their work would be judged, but such an outcome seems likely. If we know exactly what our audience expects, we are more secure about performing for them. Our profession could use a study which measures the effect of student knowledge of the criteria a teacher will use to evaluate their writing on the reduction in writing apprehension.

Shared scoring guides establish that most crucial educational relationship between teaching and evaluating. How we evaluate student work must be mediated by what we teach our students to do. Criteria scales mirror course content, consisting as they do of a review and summary of much of the material covered in a writing course. Analytic guides provide students with a point-form review and summary of the characteristics of writing their teachers most value. Holistic guides provide students with clear paragraph descriptions of those features of written discourse which their teachers view as exemplary, clear descriptions of the characteristics of unacceptable writing, and clear descriptions of writing that falls somewhere between outstanding and unacceptable. Students always want to know what is expected of them: what they need to do to get a good mark, what they need to avoid to prevent a low mark. They want to know how what they have learned relates to how they will be graded. Scoring guides provide students with this information; they establish that crucial connection between the teaching and the evaluation of writing.

Shared scoring guides encourage students to be active participants in the writing process. If their work will be judged analytically and if they have the analytic guide, students can work back and forth between their drafts and the checklist as they write and revise their work, checking off the items on the guide when they feel their essay meets those criteria. If their work will be judged holistically and if they have the holistic guide, students can try to match their work to the high-rated descriptors while avoiding the pitfalls described in the low-rated ones. The rubric tells students what they need to do to write a good essay and motivates them to meet the criteria for good writing their teacher has established for a given writing assignment. It is difficult for students to remain detached and unengaged when they have before them the evaluative criteria their teacher will apply to their writing assignment; the criteria urges them to get in the game.

Shared scoring guides force a sense of audience onto student writers. Recent composition theory has emphasized the crucial role the reader plays or should play in the writing process. Richard Fulkerson, for example, argues that a rhetorical axiology, which privileges the role of the readers, emerged in the '80s as the favored approach among influential compositionists ("Composition in the '80s"). A rhetorical axiology is based on the belief that writing is a social process, that the purpose of writing is to connect with a "discourse community," that readers influence and shape the content and style of a writer's work. "Good writing, the sort of writing that we hope to enable students to produce, is contextually adapted to, perhaps even controlled by, its audience (or discourse community) addressed or invoked or both" (417). Josephine Tarvers, similarly, notes that the "social-constructionist theory of the writing process" and its paired term, "collaborative learning," currently dominate writing theory and pedagogy (p. AIE-3). Shared scoring guides emphasize the importance of the reader's role in the composing process in that they prescribe those qualities readers will value as they read and judge a writer's work. They impel students to consider their audience as they write, and the research suggests that their writing will be better as a result.

The use of shared scoring guides complements, as well, radical composition theory which emerged in the 1990s, as an important contribution to the discipline, as composition/rhetoric specialists adapted to their field approaches their colleagues in literary theory and analysis had used for some years. Radical composition theory is primarily Marxist and/or feminist. Marxist composition theorists like James Berlin believe that power is inequitably distributed among cultures and social classes and for democracy to prevail, and for viable learning to occur, power must be redistributed. In a writing class, the teacher has more power than students have. Teachers can render writing instruction more effective and more authentic by sharing some of that power. Obviously control over grading is a primary source of teacher power, so teachers who share their evaluative criteria with their students are, at least in part, finding a pedagogical application for Marxist theory. Feminist composition theorists like Dale Bauer, Elizabeth Flynn, and Catherine Lamb advocate a feminist pedagogy based upon feminist principles. Essentially, they reject a stereotypically male approach to education based on intellectual independence, competition, and individualism in favor of a more cooperative and collaborative approach. The popularity of peer response as an instructional strategy in the writing classroom is, in part, a result of the influence of feminist educators. The shared rubric certainly fosters this atmosphere of cooperation and collaboration feminist educators value. Shared scoring guides are Marxist in their insistence that teachers share their power as evaluators; they are feminist in that they champion the pedagogical benefits of cooperation and collaboration.

Teachers also benefit from sharing their scoring guides with their students. The Wyngaard and Gehrke's study, discussed above, indicates that teachers who share evaluative criteria with their students reported that it took less time than usual for them to grade their students' work and that the evaluation process was more useful and relevant to their students (70). This conclusion, of course, stands to reason. As the research cited above suggests, students write better essays when they own the evaluative criteria, and good essays, as all English teachers know, take less time to grade than bad essays. Moreover, we can process, decode, and evaluate information that we anticipate, that has a recognizable context, more effectively than information that has only a vague context. The shared scoring guide provides teachers and students with that shared context or, at least, reminds students of the context within which their teachers expect them to communicate. If they're on the same wavelength, a reader and a writer communicate more effectively.

Shared scoring guides also act as something of a substitute for the individual teacher-student conference. Most English teachers want to conference with each of their students at least once while students are writing and revising an essay in order to monitor the students' progress, offer advice, and recommend revisions. Indeed, a study by Freedman indicates that English teachers rate the one-on-one conference as the most effective method of teaching writing. But a teacher with a hundred students doing four or five writing assignments in a semester barely has the time to conference once with each student in one semester (Freedman). A shared rubric presages much of the advice a teacher would likely give in a one-on-one conference. If teachers review the rubric with their students while the students are drafting and revising, there is at least some whole-class conferencing occurring. It is not as effective, obviously: hard copy of a list of some rules is not going to be as beneficial as a teacher taking time with each student to review the specific writing issues with which each student is struggling. But individual conferences for a class of twenty-five students will take well over six hours. Given the amount of material to be covered in a contemporary writing class, and given the typical writing teacher's workload, the considerably more efficient must trump the slightly more effective instructional strategy.

A third benefit to teachers is that the use of a clear, shared rubric reduces vexatious student complaints about their grades. Of course, any good teacher will respond willingly and openly to those students who want further explanation about the errors they made and those who want advice on how to improve subsequent writing assignments. But there are always those assertive students who want a higher grade, who demand to know exactly where, why, and how they lost every point their teacher deducted from their essay, and who threaten to take their paper to the department chair unless such specific explanation is provided to them. Such explanation is easier to provide when teachers have a scoring guide to refer to as they discuss the essay with the student and justify the grade they assigned to it. More to the point, there are fewer such complaints when students know exactly what is expected of them.

Specific evaluative criteria should accompany every writing assignment a teacher gives to his or her students. Teachers can use one of the many rubrics found within the professional literature on response or, better, design their own, perhaps using an existing rubric as a guide and model. Different types of assignments require different types of evaluative criteria: the characteristics of a persuasive essay, for example, are different from the characteristics of an effective narrative. Rubrics should also be used in peer response. Such rubrics are often framed in the form of questions: Is the essay interesting and informative? Does the essay have a beginning, a middle, and an end? Is there a thesis? Are the paragraphs developed in enough detail? Is the writing clear? Does it flow? The rubric should complement both the assignment or the activity and their rhetorical contexts.

Secondary and college writing teachers might also consider the benefits of soliciting student input in the design of the evaluative criteria to be used for a given assignment. Lee Odell recommends students take an "active role in establishing the criteria by which their writing is to be judged" (295). Writing teachers assume students understand terms like "organized," "perceptive," and "logical," when, in fact, student and teacher definitions of these terms might differ. Writing teachers must take the time to explain, discuss, and define these terms with students and within the context of a particular writing assignment. When evaluative criteria are clarified, established cooperatively, and shared, students know exactly what is expected of them and they will better understand the way their work is graded. "In all cases, the evaluation process must continually engage both teachers and students in trying to figure out what criteria are specifically appropriate for the task at hand" (295).

Edward White, in his readable book *Teaching and Assessing Writing*, recommends writing teachers share their scoring guides with their students early in the writing process, "so that they know from the outset the standards for judgment to which they will be subject" (19). Like Odell, he also suggests that teachers solicit input from their students in the design of the scoring guide. "Teachers who use scoring guides in this way spend more time working with students as they write their papers, since the standards for performance are clear and public and the students are more ready to seek help in meeting them" (19). When students have the scoring guide, they feel included. They feel they are collaborating with their teachers in achieving the goals of the course. This sense of inclusion is heightened further when students have a hand in developing the scoring guide. They have a real sense of responsibility to try their best to meet the criteria which they have helped establish, in the same way workers who own the company will work harder to make the company viable. Effective writing teachers, White argues, include criteria scales with their assignments. "The students should receive a description of the purpose of the assignment, its format, and the criteria that the teacher will use in responding to it" (25).

Research, reviewed above, indicates that students who know the criteria upon which their work will be evaluated write more effectively than students who do not own that criteria. Will writing performance improve even more if students have a hand in designing the evaluative criteria? Will such students write more effectively than students who have simply been given a prescribed rubric? There is, as yet, no research which ventures to answer that question. Our profession needs a study comparing the effect on student writing of a prescribed rubric with the effect of a rubric students have had a share in designing.

We do know that the use of shared scoring guides is an effective instructional strategy in the composition classroom. Indeed, composition theory and research suggest that every writing assignment that is going to be evaluated, assessed, and/or graded should come with its own rubric, which explains clearly the specific criteria upon which the writing will be judged. Teachers should explain and discuss the rubrics, whatever type they choose, carefully with their students. Placement tests should include the grading criteria and proctors should extend by a few minutes the time they spend going over the instructions for the placement essay, so they can explain and discuss the rubrics with students who are writing the placement essay. Rubrics should be used in peer conferencing sessions to provide a clear focus for students to constructively critique each other's work. Students, especially in higher grades and college, should write better essays, take the writing process more seriously, and enjoy writing more if they are allowed to participate in the design of the criteria scale. The use of shared scoring guides complements the current thinking of some of our leaders in the English education community. Shared rubrics empower students, they urge students to become active participants in the writing process, and they substantiate the connections among teaching, learning, and assessment.

Chapter Fifteen
GRADING AS A TEACHING STRATEGY

We grade our students' written work in order to determine the extent to which students have mastered an aspect of the content of the course and to assess our students' ability to express that knowledge fluently. We also grade our students' written work as a way of encouraging and teaching them to improve their writing. We correct errors and offer suggestions for revision to help students do better the next time they are given a writing assignment. Grading is not only a method of assessment, it is also a pedagogical strategy. The purpose of this chapter is to discuss some methods we can use to ensure that grading supports and enhances learning, to ensure that those hours we spend every week evaluating our students' written work will be time well spent, because it will help us realize the goals of the courses we teach. To grade written work effectively, we should:

- Comment in an honest but positive and encouraging voice;
- Insist students reflect upon our comments;
- Match the grading method to the assignment;
- Establish clear evaluative criteria and share them with our students;
- Grade a draft;
- Grade with colleagues.

Comment in a Positive, Encouraging Voice

Students learn more effectively when teacher feedback is positive and encouraging. "Positive and encouraging" does not mean dishonest, nor is it a phrase meant to sanction insincere flattery. It means praising what is good about a paper and criticizing what is bad, but doing so constructively. It is the difference between comments like "Huh,???" "nonsense!" "buy a dictionary!" "this bibliography is a farce," "obviously I've taught you nothing"—all teacher comments that I, as the director of a writing program of a large state university have seen recently—and comments like "David, you need to express your thesis more clearly;" "Joan, you need to proofread with greater care;" "remember the connotation of a word is as important as its denotation;" "you need to research your topic more thoroughly;" "please see me after class today." Regrettably, the tone of the former set of comments is prevalent in grader feedback.

Nancy Sommers and her colleagues studied the grading practices of thirty-five college writing teachers, focusing on "comments teachers write to motivate revisions" (340) in student texts. They found that teacher comments were often hostile and mean-spirited (340). Connors and Glenn, similarly, in their review of the research, found evidence of "harsh or disrespectful comments that usurp student control over the text" (105). Writing teachers, at least when they are grading papers, often assume the persona of a drill sergeant, ordering their recruits to "be precise,"

89

"do more research," "think," "consult your text," "elaborate," and exhorting them to stop being "wordy," "colloquial," "vague," and "awkward."

Theory and research on the overall efficacy of comments is mixed (see Hillocks 219; Horvath 248) but there is general agreement that students will be better motivated to produce competent texts when teachers praise those aspects of their work that deserve praise and criticize weaknesses constructively, in a voice that indicates the student's work can and will improve with some extra effort. Horvath cites the work of Robert Gee and Carl Rogers in support of his or her contention that

> the evaluator's role as motivator is crucial, for it is in this role that the teacher speaks as the students' sincere (if somewhat artificial) friend, applauding their successes, urging them to look forward to the effects certain remediations will have on their work, setting goals to strive toward, encouraging risk-taking, fostering the desire to write more and to write better. (248)

Students will appreciate the written comments on their graded papers, will learn from them and will be motivated to revise and improve their work if the grader's voice is positive and encouraging.

Other research suggests that we need to be especially careful in formulating our summative (or "terminal"—a word I don't like because of its connotations) comments at the end of student papers. Students tend to skim marginal comments, which often baffle them, but they usually read carefully the summative comment, which they consider a personal note their teacher has sent them. In his or her study, Sarah Freedman found that the aspect of evaluation students value most highly—more than individual conferences with their teacher, comments written on drafts, or evaluation of any kind from their peers (78)—are thoughtful written comments on the final draft of their papers.

Connors and Glenn argue that summative comments

> must document the strengths and weaknesses of a paper, let students know whether they responded well to your assignment, help create a psychological environment in which the students are willing to revise or write again, encourage and discourage specific writing behaviors, and set specific goals that you think the student can meet. (104)

Connors and Lunsford, similarly, suggest that the summative comment should present the teacher's impression of the paper as a whole, emphasizing the extent to which the thesis is relevant to the assignment and well supported. In a "serious yet interested tone" (qtd. in Connors and Glenn 105), graders should praise the good aspects of the paper and offer constructive criticism to improve the weaknesses. The grader should point out improvements made over a previous assignment and suggestions to further improve subsequent assignments. The grader need not reiterate marginal comments, which usually highlight grammatical and mechanical errors. A good summative comment, according to Connors and Lunsford, is between 100 and 150 words in length (105). Their own research revealed that the average summative comment is about thirty-one words in length, which may be less desirable but which is a more realistic goal for most teachers, given their heavy workloads.

Insist Students Reflect Upon Written Comments

The marginal and summative comments we write on our students' papers are of little use unless students read them, consider them, reflect upon them. There are several strategies a teacher can employ to make certain students heed the comments the teacher has so painstakingly written throughout the students' papers.

One strategy is to ask students, immediately after they have received back a graded paper, to make two lists, one of which describes three weaknesses in the paper, according to the teacher's comments, the other of which describes three strengths. The teacher then asks the students to put a star beside the one weakness and the one strength they consider most significant. Next, the teacher goes around the room and asks each student to read out the weakness he or she listed. The teacher, and other students, can comment on ways to overcome this weakness while the student drafts the next assignment. Then, the teacher goes around the room again, this time asking students to read out the main strength they listed. This exercise reinforces instruction in the elements of good writing and affords the teacher the opportunity to explain why the strength each student named is an important component of sound writing. It is, in my experience, one of the most effective whole-class exercises a composition teacher can undertake with his or her students.

We can, as well, ask students to write a written response to our end comment. Some teachers have their students write in their journals a no-holds-barred response to the teacher's comments immediately after the teacher returns graded work. We can also ask students to write a letter, at the end of the semester, in which they detail their growth and progress as writers, as reflected in the accumulated teacher response to their work. Such assignments—a staple of portfolio evaluation—force students to attend to our evaluative comments and help them understand that grading is a rehabilitative and not a punitive enterprise.

Match the Grading Method to the Assignment

Most competent and effective written texts have ISCE: intelligence, substance, clarity, and energy. Effective writing reflects a sound knowledge of its subject, provides enough information for the readers to go on, is well organized, and has a style that animates (that does not impair) its content. Writing, especially writing done in school and college, needs good ideas, ones that are interesting, informative, and well researched. Those ideas need substance, that is, they need to be developed in enough detail to satisfy the needs and expectations of readers. The text needs to be clear, a function of a sound structure, cohesion, good grammar, good spelling, proper punctuation. And good writing has energy, a distinctive voice, syntactic variety, a bit of flair. These are traits common to most sound written texts. But since writing contexts differ, since different assignments call for different things and different readers expect different types of information, textual style and content will vary from one text to the next. Textual variety calls for some variety in evaluation methods.

We should, in other words, match our method of grading to the assignment. There are basically three methods of grading available to us. We can respond with marginal and terminal comments but without assigning a letter or a numeric grade. We can grade holistically, a method which reduces written comments but which does require a letter or a numeric grade. Or we can grade analytically, a method which requires both extensive written comments, marginal and terminal, and a letter or numeric grade. Each method has its place in the writing curriculum.

The response-with-no-grade method is best suited to personal writing, especially the kind students typically do in their journals. Students often express their values and attitudes in their journals, often use their journals to puzzle out their personal problems, to express their aspirations and their fears about the future. To assign an alpha or numeric value to such writing seems rather callous, and, indeed, might silence or at least inhibit our students' self-expression, one of the main goals of journal writing. Teachers usually prefer to make written responses especially to the content, occasionally to the style of the journal, but to avoid judging its quality.

Holistic grading is most effective for extemporaneous essays including placement tests, in-class assignments, and final exams. A holistic system consists usually of four, five, or six paragraphs, each of which describes the qualities and characteristics of a typical student essay at various levels of competence. A four-point holistic scale, for example, would consist of four paragraphs, one of which describes the qualities of an excellent essay written in response to a particular extemporaneous essay assignment, one of which describes the qualities of a good essay, one of which describes the qualities of an average essay, and one the qualities of a poor essay. The paragraphs are numbered from one to four, with a four representing an excellent essay, a three a good essay, a two an average essay, and a one a poor essay. The grader gives each essay the number of the paragraph which best describes the qualities of the essay being graded. Holistic scales are norm-referenced, which means the quality of an essay is judged in relationship to the qualities of the other essays being graded. Holistic grading does not penalize, to the same extent as other methods do, errors caused by time constraints. It also obviates the need for comprehensive comments because the paragraph descriptors—which the test-takers should be given before they take the test—take the place of comments, at least to an extent.

Analytic grading works best for written assignments completed over a period of time, anywhere from a few days to a few weeks. Analytic scales are criterion-referenced, which means the grader establishes a set of criteria upon which the work will be judged. Essays are evaluated based upon the presence or the absence of these criteria. The grader flags each error or lapse in style, explains the nature of the error (or praises a positive feature of the work) in a marginal comment, composes a terminal comment describing the quality of the essay as a whole, then gives the essay a letter grade or a numerical value which is a measure of its quality. The analytic scale might simply be a checklist of anywhere from a dozen to twenty criteria the grader will be looking for as he or she evaluates the students' texts. Or it might be a grid which consists of a number of key traits of good writing followed by a set of boxes labeled "weak," "average," "good," "excellent." The grader checks the appropriate box. Students prefer to have their work, especially work they completed outside of class, graded analytically, because it gives them a clear picture of the specific strengths and weaknesses of the writing assignment being graded. They might learn, for example, that their sentence structure is weak, their organization good, their diction is good, their paragraph development average, their thesis excellent. Marginal and summative comments provide additional explanation. Students know exactly where they failed and where they succeeded, what to do and what not to do to improve their next writing assignment.

Establish Clear Evaluative Criteria and Share Them with Students

Grading supports teaching if teachers establish clear evaluative criteria they will use to judge student writing and share those criteria with their students. Indeed, research suggests a positive correlation between a student's knowledge of evaluative criteria and the grade the student gets on an essay to which that evaluative criteria is applied. Hillocks reviewed eleven studies done between 1963 and 1982 on the use of criteria scales and feedback sheets to improve student writing (156-160). Participants in the studies ranged in level from sixth grade to first-year college. In these studies, an experimental group was given a list of the criteria upon which a particular writing assignment would be judged; a control group was not. In most cases, teachers discussed the criteria with their students and encouraged them to comply with the criteria as they worked on their writing assignments. "Most of the studies involved found statistically significant differences between students using the sets of criteria and those taught through some other technique" (56). After reviewing the studies, Hillocks selected the best six, combined their results and evaluated these results statistically, using a sophisticated technique called a meta-analysis. He reports a mean effect size (a measure of overall difference in performance between experimental and control groups in all six studies combined) of a respectable .36. This rating makes the use of shared scoring guides the second most effective instructional strategy Hillocks investigated, second only to inquiry and ahead of sentence combining, model analysis, free writing, and grammar instruction.

In a well-designed study, Lamm investigated the efficacy of three instructional methods for teaching argumentative writing to college freshmen:

- the study of exemplary models of writing,
- the use of criteria scales, and
- revision which, in this study, involved using a criteria scale to revise a writing sample, which was not written by the students doing the revision exercise.

Two teachers used each of the three treatments in separate writing classes; in other words, six writing classes, a total of 102 students, participated in the study. Results of the study indicate that criteria scales are the most effective of the three methods studied for teaching writing. The effect size for models was 0.19; for revision, 0.48, and for scales 0.54. One instructor's Scales students registered a huge effect size, in excess of a full standard deviation (1.095). Lamm speculates that scales "may offer a better bridge [than models] from declarative to procedural knowledge" (6). In other words, the study of exemplary models of writing teach students <u>what</u> is effective and ineffective (declarative knowledge) but not <u>how</u> to make their own writing more effective (procedural knowledge). Scales do both. Lamm's study also indicates that female students benefit more from the application of scales to their writing than male students do. He also believes scales work especially well for argumentative writing, which makes more intellectual demands on students than other rhetorical modes do.

Wyngaard and Gehrke also experimented with the use of criteria scales to improve student writing. They used a type of analytic rubric, known as a primary trait scale, which focused on three aspects of effective writing: openings, focus, and "showing not telling." They described the qualities of excellent, good, adequate, and ineffective writing across each trait. They discussed the rubrics with their students and gave students written descriptions of the rubrics to help them assess their own work. Finally, they used the rubrics themselves to assess the students' writing. Their study indicates that the use of rubrics is an effective way to improve student writing.

Stoddard and MacArthur found that shared scoring guides improved the narrative writing of learning-disabled students. The seventh- and eighth-grade students who participated in their study worked in pairs to assist each other in revising their writing. The rubric, which they used, prompted the students to examine and critique the parts, order, details, and clarity of each other's narratives (85). As the rubric indicates, the researchers were interested more in substantive rather than mechanical improvement to the students' writing. Students were thoroughly and carefully trained in using the rubrics effectively. Over the course of the study, student writing improved significantly, confirming the efficacy of the use of the rubric. "Improvement for individual students from baseline to posttest ranged from 2.6 to 5.5 points on an eight-point scale" (91).

It is not difficult to understand how and why shared criteria support and enhance learning. Any set of evaluative criteria will be a summary of at least part of the content of a composition course. Holistic scales provide students with a set of paragraphs, detailing various levels of writing competence for a given assignment. Students can write in the context of the scale, trying to match their essay to the qualities described in the paragraph with the highest rating, while trying to avoid the qualities described in the paragraph with the lowest rating. With an analytic scale, similarly, students can move back and forth between the criteria for good writing listed on the scale and their own work and revise in such a way that their essay matches the criteria listed. Students must own the criteria their teacher uses to evaluate their written work. Shared criteria scales reify both instruction in and the evaluation of student writing.

Grade a Draft

We should respond to at least one draft of a student's assignment before we grade the final product. Since most English teachers now teach writing as a process, it stands to reason that teachers should also respond to the work in process, not just to the finished product. As part of his or her study of the attitudes of 715 secondary school students to teacher response, Sarah Freedman also polled the teachers and found that most of them rated in-process response as one of the most valuable aspects of essay assessment.

Leonard and Joanne Podis also suggest writing teachers respond to the successive drafts of their students' work. This suggestion may be idealistic, given the work load most English teachers have, but the concept is certainly laudatory, and a response, even, to the penultimate draft would be beneficial. The Podises urge teachers to "undertake close readings of student drafts in order to pinpoint rhetorical or structural problems that might signal legitimate intentions rather than simply failure or inadequacy" (367). While grading a draft, teachers should try to "comprehend the mental process that underlies some evidence of difficulty in creating a discourse" (367). An error is not simply a mistake; it is a clue to the writer's actual intention. If we can decode the error, we can understand more clearly the writer's purpose and offer better advice on how to improve the final product.

Brooke Horvath recommends we always grade as if we are grading a draft, that we always view grading as formative as opposed to summative. Summative assessment "treats a text as a finished product and the author's writing ability as at least momentarily fixed" (244). An alpha or numeric grade which establishes the worth of the paper or which measures the quality of a paper by comparing it to others is the hallmark of summative assessment. Formative assessment "treats a text as part of an ongoing process of skills acquisition and improvement, recognizing that what is being responded to is not a fixed but a developing entity" (244). Summative assessment appropriates the student's text, implying it is being measured against some ideal text the teacher has in mind and against which the teacher is measuring the quality of the student's text. Formative evaluation measures the extent to which the student is achieving the aims he or she has, herself, established for fulfilling this assignment.

Horvath's argument is enticing, if, ultimately, idealistic. At some point, the student wants a number or a letter and the system (usually) demands it. It is not always wrong, moreover, for a teacher to co-opt a student's text, though much recent composition theory regards such co-opting as sinful. But students can go off track in responding to an assignment, and it is the teacher's job to get students to fulfill the requirements of a given assignment if the goals of the course are to be met. Professors in other disciplines will certainly co-opt their students' texts. And, in the real world, supervisors, employers, department chairs, deans, lawyers, and others will return a proposal, a letter, a memo, a report not done to specifications. Indeed, it is because the final product will be judged that it is so important to assess a draft or two of a work in progress.

Grade with Colleagues

We should, about once a semester, get together with our colleagues and grade a set of student writing assignments collaboratively. The pedagogical benefits of the evaluative process multiply when students get feedback from a variety of expert readers. Moreover, students can be somewhat more secure in the knowledge that their work is being graded objectively, if more than one trained professional is evaluating it.

Independent grading is, to a considerable extent, a subjective process, though many teachers wish it were not so. English teachers want, to use Scharton's phrase, "a catholic belief system" (59), which will, once and for all, prescribe for us the criteria to use to judge good academic writing. Anson, similarly, claims that English teachers want "some key method, informed by theory and predictable in outcome" to "lessen some of the bewildering complexity that reading students' work inevitably calls into play" (375). In fact, the evidence suggests that the key which will unlock the secret of grading consensus will never be cut.

Diederich, French, and Carlton, in a now infamous study, asked over fifty readers from six different fields to evaluate, on a nine-point scale, 300 first-year composition essays. Specifically, they asked each grader to divide the 300 essays into three piles—one for above-average essays, one for average essays, and one for below-average essays. Then they asked the graders to again divide each pile in the same way, so that, in the end, there were nine piles, each one supposedly containing essays of about equal quality. Every single essay was put in at least five of the piles, and one-third of them were placed in all nine piles (in Wolcott 62). What one reader judged to be outstanding work, another judged to be atrocious.

In *Twelve Readers Reading*, Straub and Lunsford describe the grading practices of twelve composition teachers, several of whom are among the most prominent scholars in the field. The researchers studied and analyzed the marginal and terminal comments the teachers made as they graded first-year composition essays on such topics as seat belt laws, the legalization of drugs, bass fishing, street gangs, waitressing, and a John Cougar rock concert. The researchers chose not to have the graders assign an alpha or numeric grade to the essays—something of a cop-out since most schools require grades—but they did thoroughly analyze the comments and the teachers' responding styles. Nearly every evaluation of every essay reveals some disagreement among the markers. Phrases like "quite different manners and tones of response" (21); "disagree quite markedly" (34); "differ significantly" (78); "opinions differ as to just how good Elizabeth's essay is" (92); "Our readers do not agree on what should be done with this essay" (128) appear in most of the summaries of the graders' responses. Even the experts cannot agree on the quality of a typical student essay.

In "Reflective Reading: Developing Thoughtful Ways to Respond to Students' Writing" Chris Anson presents a fascinating example of the extent to which English teachers can disagree about the quality of a student essay, if they disagree about the relative importance of form and content. The essay in question was written by Leang, a young Cambodian refugee (Anson 376). It is a harrowing, fascinating, and moving account of what his life was like in communist Cambodia, before he escaped to America. The ideas in the essay are well developed; the paragraphing is not bad. But the first sentence reads: "Thanks God for let me have my life still, also thanks for let me have my little brother too, plus my older one and sisters" (376), and nearly every other sentence in the essay contains similar errors in grammar, sentence structure, and mechanics—errors ESL students habitually make.

The stickler for Standard English says this about Leang's essay:

It's clear that Leang is misplaced. Something went wrong in the diagnostic or advising system. He belongs in an ESL class, where he would get the kind of help he needs as a non-native speaker, especially with the surface mechanics and grammar. (Anson 380)

But the teacher who values creativity and inspiration says this:

I'm incredibly moved by this account. In fact, the story is so authentic that cleaning up the errors makes it too Anglo, too fake. There is something compelling about the voice, the voice of a real refugee. I want to react in all my original horror, to be moved, because the story is moving and Leang should know it. (Anson 381)

And a teacher with a political agenda, Anson speculates, might criticize Leang's essay because it endorses "an American system that has its own share of atrocities both national and international" (383).

Age, race, and gender, and personal values might also influence grading. Reader response theory asserts that readers filter texts through the lens of their social class, their ethnicity, gender, values and ideals, sexual orientation, and age, and that readers judge texts, at least in part, accordingly. There is more theory than there is research on the influence of such factors. Still, it is possible that stereotypical gender roles might influence grading. Women and men might be more favorably disposed to different topics and might tend to grade essays on preferred topics more generously. Men might prefer a strong authoritative voice; women a more moderate voice (Brody). Women might prefer a creative writing style, men, a more prosaic one. Women might give a higher grade to a narrative essay, men to a persuasive essay. Similarly, older teachers might privilege certain topics and genres more than younger teachers do. African American teachers might be more predisposed to a certain writing style than their colleagues are. Gay/lesbian teachers might be more predisposed to certain topics and genres than their colleagues are. Pro-choice markers might downgrade a pro-life essay because they do not agree with the student's point of view. A teacher who belongs to the NRA might penalize an essay about the need for gun control.

There is some evidence, even, that suggests that factors peripherally related to professional competence or personal identity can influence grading. Teachers tend to give higher grades to papers they grade at home than to papers they grade during a marking session at work with other teachers (Wolcott 64). Apparently, English teachers fear censor from their colleagues if they appear too soft. In collaborative grading sessions, demanding, even uncompromising standards seem to be prized. Similarly, teachers might be less generous with their grades when they are tired and more generous when they are well rested; less generous when they are in a bad mood and more generous when they are in good spirits. Overworked English teachers have to grade rapidly and might be more or less generous than they would be if they had the time they need to grade fairly and objectively.

Now collaborative grading sessions are not going to supersede personal identity, but, to an extent, at least, collaborative grading sessions will control subjective variables. Such sessions typically begin with a discussion of the criteria graders will apply to the writing assignments they are assessing. Graders will usually reach consensus about these criteria, a process which assures some measure of objectivity when these criteria are used to assess student writing. More-over, group members can alert fellow group members to possible biases that may be affecting their grading practices, and group members can urge each other to put aside these biases in the interest of objective evaluation.

Certainly there are leaders in the field who are critical of collaborative grading, who argue that the objectivity collaborative grading achieves is artificial because teachers alter their personal standards and beliefs in the interest of group harmony. Davida Charney (in Wolcott 61) suggests that teachers might alter their practice as a result of the training they go through to "calibrate" their grading standards. Peter Elbow argues that the objectivity collaborative grading achieves "is not a measure of how texts are valued by real readers in natural settings, but only of how they are valued in artificial settings with imposed agreements" (396). Pat Belanoff (in Wolcott 61) is the most critical, calling the training process a form of brainwashing and warning against a process that produces reliability only at the cost of validity.

But inter-rater reliability, a measure of the extent to which graders agree on the quality of a sample of written discourse, does increase when teachers grade collaboratively. And the testimony of participating teachers refutes the argument that they have abandoned their own educational philosophies in the interest of group harmony (Wolcott 70). Collaborative grading is rare because of the logistical difficulties of getting a group of busy professionals together in one place for any sustained period of time. Most student writing is and will continue to be graded independently. Students are hardly disadvantaged if one of the four or five essays they write for a course is graded by a group. Indeed their writing is likely to improve if they get feedback from a variety of expert readers. Moreover, those student writers who feel teachers will downgrade their work if their teachers do not agree with the ideas they express in their work, might be appeased, knowing that their work is being evaluated by several teachers, not all of whom share the possible biases of their teacher.

Teachers also benefit, of course, from collaborative grading, primarily as a result of discussing grading practices with colleagues and sharing ideas about effective methods. "Sharing such reflections," notes Anson, "not only exposes us to different response strategies. . . . , but also helps us to formulate theoretical and practical justifications for the decisions we make" (388). We acquire, in the process, "a larger repertoire of response strategies and a clearer, more informed understanding of how to use such strategies in the classroom" (388).

Grading papers is exhausting and time consuming. It can be depressing, as well, if we are uncertain about the extent to which the process is improving our students' writing ability. The guidelines for effective grading presented here won't make grading any less exhausting or time consuming. But if we follow these guidelines, we can be more confident that our exhaustive effort is having beneficial effects and that our valuable time is being well spent.

Chapter Sixteen
COMPUTERS AND THE TEACHING OF WRITING

The Affirmative

It is hard to overstate the influence the computer has had on the learning and teaching of writing. The computer has changed the nature of the writing process, making research, drafting, revising, and editing faster and more efficient. It has changed the way we teach writing, giving us new ways to respond to student writing, new rhetorical genres to teach, new ways of delivering instruction, and new support systems in the form of online writing labs and textbook websites, where students can go for additional support and further instruction. Thanks to the computer, students write better today than they did in the age of the typewriter.

Computers improve student writing because they facilitate most of the components of the composing process. The editing process, for example, is simpler and less time consuming thanks to word processing programs. With their built-in software, in the form of spell checks and grammar checks, sophisticated enough to flag such sentence-level errors as passive voice, sentence fragments, and run-on sentences, word processors reduce the number of editing errors student writers are prone to make (Kiefer and Moran). Unlike a textbook, which simply exhorts writers to avoid errors in spelling and grammar, the computer is interactive—it flags errors and offers correct alternatives, implemented with a click of a mouse.

The computer also facilitates revision (Sudol), easily allowing writers to add additional sentences to paragraphs and, with the highlight, cut, and copy functions, to move entire paragraphs from one section of a text to another. Students who need to revise by adding ideas to support a point or develop an argument can access software designed to help writers generate essay content or search for additional information on a website on the Internet. Students who are uncertain about effective revision strategies can learn them through software programs designed to teach effective revision practices (Barton 68). Indeed, while they are composing, students can pause to access a video, perhaps an animated demonstration, explaining the components of the writing process and how best to marshal them. Or, they can call up an annotated model text and use it to access the extent to which their own work matches the model. When the time comes to cite their sources, they can click on to a bibliography tool, which will walk them through the process, correcting their errors as they proceed.

Computers improve student writing because they support the social nature of written discourse, and writing is as much a social as a cognitive transaction. Writers invoke cognitive processes to create a text, but that cognition is worth the effort only if it is mediated by the author's sense of the needs and expectations of the readers for whom the text is intended. To stress the need to make text reader friendly, most writing teachers set aside time for peer review of drafts, during which students read and constructively criticize each other's draft or a portion of it. There is some evidence to suggest that networked peer conferencing is more effective than face-to-face conferencing. In his study of the effect of electronic feedback on the writing ability of L2 students, Tuzi found that e-feedback was more effective than oral feedback in encouraging students to revise their work. Duin and Hansen cite studies that suggest that there is greater participation among students critiquing each other's work online (102). Because the teacher is not present, in front of the classroom, directing, perhaps co-opting the peer-review process, students feel empowered and are more inclined to participate. Teachers in networked sections participate more than they do in non-networked classrooms, but more as guides and facilitators than infallible experts. And, working online, teachers interact more with students who need help the most, than do instructors not teaching networked sections (102).

Networked peer review offers another significant benefit. Students—women and minority students, especially—who feel intimidated and are, hence, silenced, in face-to-face peer conferencing can participate openly in computer conferences, taking advantage of the anonymity the network imposes upon them (Barton 71). Computers are great equalizers, narrowing the rhetorical gap between minority and dominant-culture students and giving all students an equal rhetorical voice. On networks, students can even peer-review the work of students in other countries or simply communicate with them, an activity which, as Wresh reports, fosters understanding and builds friendships across cultures (188).

The increasing popularity of the collaborative writing assignment represents another way in which social constructivist theory is influencing curriculum, and here, again, students who are technologically literate will have an advantage. The collaborative project is a mainstay of corporate America, into whose offices many of our students will eventually settle. Collaborative projects are increasingly conducted at least partly online, since the expertise needed to sustain them may be spread across the country. Students who learn how to work online on a collaborative project are preparing for success in many of the careers they decide to pursue. And, given the creative options technology offers, the collaborative project can result in a presentation or a "text," consisting of a dazzling mix of audio, visual, and print information, more interesting and insightful than a text consisting only of print.

Computers improve student writing because they motivate students to write; students enjoy composing on computers more than they enjoy composing with pen and paper (LeBlanc 29). Students are more likely to visit their university writing center, and to feel less stigmatized doing so, if the center is equipped with computers (Palmquist). Indeed, students enjoy even those writing classes that demand significant skill in using technology. Surveying forty-two of her students from three sections of a first-year composition program that relies heavily on technology, Jones reports that 55 percent of her students rated technology one of the best liked aspects of the course (289). They especially enjoyed creating their own individual Web pages and experienced that "wow moment" (292), rare in a first-year composition class, when they accessed for the first time the Web pages they had designed in class.

Computers improve student writing because they provide so many more opportunities for students to write and more occasions to write in new genres and various voices. Email tends to be informal, hence the rules that govern academic writing are often overlooked, but, even so, the communication is occurring in writing and may positively influence other forms of writing, given, especially, the volume of email students now send and receive. Whole-class discussion, easily and increasingly conducted online in writing, is less casual than email, still conversational in tone, but more formal in expression. Students can read and respond to each other's drafts online, an exercise that can demand carefully structured, sophisticated language, as group members must comment intelligently on each other's work, writing honestly while, at the same time, diplomatically enough to avoid offending classmates. Moreover, commenting, in writing, on the efficacy of a written text, is a complex process that fosters that meta-cognitive and meta-linguistic awareness that develop writing ability. Finally, students now can write and submit hypertext essays, e-folios and e-zines, the most impressive of all of the new genres the computer allows. Working in hypertext, students provide readers with so much more than mere print, with audio and video presentations and Internet links that can do so much to enrich and amplify a writing assignment. Techies argue that writing teachers have a responsibility to take students beyond print, because multi-media presentations are common now in business and industry. The meaning of "effective communicator" has expanded to include the ability to put together a multi-media presentation.

Computers improve student writing because they make it so much easier for students to research a topic. Without leaving their bedrooms or dorms, students can log on to the Internet and their library website and quickly access, download, and print much of the research they will need to complete a writing assignment. Inevitably, hypertexts have links to other related hypertexts, freeing students "to wander through an array of connected texts, graphics, and commentary, to explore and create topical paths of association at will" (Charney 240). English teachers often complain about the insipidity of their students' writing, but student writing lacks substance often because library research is so time consuming. With a connected computer, students can research a topic in less than half the time it used to take.

Computers improve student writing because they make it easier for teachers to respond to their students' writing. Students can easily send, as an email attachment, early drafts of a work in progress. Using a built-in editing package (the "track changes" feature of Microsoft Word, for example), teachers can offer suggestions to help students revise their work. Computers complement the process approach to the teaching of writing because they make it so easy for teachers to intervene and offer suggestions about a draft in progress before students submit their final products. Such intervention does not have to take place during the teacher's spare or office hours, which are often scheduled at times inconvenient to students. Electronically connected to their students, teachers are nearly always open for business. Electronic feedback also tends to be more substantive. Since word processing programs correct spelling, grammar, and other editing errors, teachers can concentrate their advice on the content, development of ideas, and overall structure of their students' written work.

The Negative

It is hard to overstate the influence the computer has had on the teaching and learning of writing. The computer has changed the nature of the writing process, making research, drafting, revising, and editing faster and more efficient. It has changed the way we teach writing, giving us new ways to respond to student writing, new rhetorical genres to teach, new ways of delivering instruction, and new support systems in the form of online writing labs and textbook websites where students can go for additional support and further instruction. Yet student writing is no better today than it was in the age of the typewriter; the computer revolution has had no beneficial effect on the overall quality of student writing.

A computer does not make it any easier for a writer to invoke, appropriately and infallibly, the components of the writing process. Spell checks may facilitate editing, though if the misspelling is egregious, the word processing program will not be able to offer the correct spelling. Grammar checks also help some, but they will flag sentences that are correct and miss errors that should be corrected. The program which I am using for this chapter, for example, identifies this sentence—That the computer revolution has radically altered the way students learn and teachers teach is no longer the subject of intense debate—as a fragment, but it is a complete sentence. It does not flag this sentence—Neither one of my English professors are very energetic—though "are" should be "is." David Dobrin (in Walhstrom 179-80) has examined a number grammar check programs and confirms that they will, on occasion, flag errors that aren't and miss errors that are.

Similarly, computers may facilitate revision but they cannot force writers to revise. Revision is a cognitive not a technical skill, so students won't necessarily revise more simply because they can move text around easily (Daiute). Colavito reviewed research which indicates that computer-generated texts are longer but not necessarily better than texts not written with a computer (153). Nor does the research indicate that writers revise more when using a word processor.

Computers are anti-social and, as such, work against the social constructivist approach to teaching writing, the theory that, at the present time, most influences composition pedagogy. Peer conferencing, peer review of drafts of a work in progress, is the most common pedagogical manifestation of social constructivist theory; most teachers make time for students to read and to respond constructively to drafts of each other's work. In networked classes, students peer conference online, in writing. Duin and Hansen report that online feedback is often off topic. Students preferred to talk about their personal lives and to socialize with classmates rather than comment constructively on each other's work. Thompson (in Duin and Hansen 104) found that students had less time to respond to each other's writing because of the time it took them to read each other's comments. They became complacent; the teacher had to motivate and encourage them; and, as a consequence, it was she not her students who contributed the most to online conferencing sessions (104).

Peer conferencing is more authentic and beneficial in face-to-face discussions among a small group of students, where nonverbal cues can be processed and comments that seem harsh and undiplomatic can quickly and easily be explained and corrected. In a networked environment, peer conferencing is a cumbersome and detached process; students frequently complain about feeling isolated from their teacher and classmates (Peterson). The experience is rather like having a dinner party online. It can be done. Participants agree on what they will prepare for dinner, share the recipe online, then bring their wine and dinner to their monitor to chat online about its quality and about the various social, cultural, familial interests they share. But, like knowledge, food is more palatable when it is shared in a genuinely communal context, not in one inhibited by a keyboard and a monitor.

Collaborative writing is another increasingly popular activity in writing classes and another activity inhibited rather than enhanced with computer technology. Collaborative writing assignments are often sabotaged by group dynamics. One group member slacks off and lets the others do the work; another co-opts the role of leader without the assent of others; group members form alliances with those to whom they are drawn and ignore others. Throw technology into the mix and the problems increase. One group member is far more adept with the computer than others are and grows impatient acting as the group's technology consultant. Another uses software incompatible with programs others use, causing additional delays and frustration. Another simply cannot get the hang of the complex telecommunications system needed to undertake the assignment; another refuses even to try. These are just some of the problems Janis Forman reports in his or her study of four groups of UCLA students charged with the task of producing a collaborative business report and provided with state-of-the art computer equipment to expedite the process (137-39).

Myers-Breslin, similarly, found that students cooperate but do not necessarily collaborate when working together online. Her study revealed that each member of an online group wrote a separate section of a paper and the sections were simply combined to form a whole paper. Students did not study and analyze each other's contributions and attempt to integrate and synthesize individual contributions to create a unified and coherent text, the real purpose of a collaborative exercise (163). Hawisher and Selfe also subdue the enthusiasm many English teachers have for collaboration in networked classrooms, noting that students tend to interact with peers in nonsubstantive ways online, often because creative interaction was stymied by rigid rules and regulations established by the teacher. Collaborative writing is challenging enough for a group sitting together around a table, let alone for a group whose members are working in isolation, hunched over a keyboard, and connected only in impersonal cyberspace.

Social contructivist theorists are committed, as well, to democratizing literacy, to improving the reading and writing skills of minority students and to giving a rhetorical voice to those the system tends to silence—minority students again, and women. Some turn to the computer as an ally, in the hope that technology will help bring the literacy abilities of minority students up to par with dominant-culture students and will give an equal rhetorical voice to all students, regardless of race, class, or gender. What they have found, instead, is that the demographics for computer use and ownership indicate that computers do not redistribute but consolidate power. Of even greater concern is that computer interfaces can recapitulate racism, sexism and social class inequities by representing knowledge as hierarchical, rational, logical, and hence, white and masculine and by validating, through their language and icons, the values of corporate America.

Minority students are less likely to own a computer (Forman) and when they use them in school, they use remedial skills-and-drills programs anathema to social constructivists. More men than women own, use, and develop expertise in the use of computers (Forman 133), because women are more likely to be intimidated by technology (Wahlstrom 175). Wahlstrom suggests that the reason why networks have not had the salutary effect on writing that techies thought they would is because they are almost always designed by men, and, as such, reflect a rational, objective, impersonal, and quantifiable bias, not conducive to the development of writing ability. Perhaps if the systems were more interactive, people-oriented, and less quantifiable, as they would likely be if they were designed by women, they might be more effective (176).

Computers are valorized because they provide more opportunities for students to write in a wide variety of genres and in a variety of voices. But teachers would rather not see the rhetorical conventions of the typical freshman's email, which proudly flouts the conventions of Standard English, creep in to their students' essays. Online peer conferencing may be conducted in writing but any gain in writing practice afforded by online peer review is offset by the impersonal and sometimes hostile nature of the remote written comment, which often makes students feel they are being "flamed" by classmates. Peer review is more effective when mediated by the tact and diplomacy afforded by body language and tone of voice that in-person conferences allow. Hypertext is lauded as the ultimate computer-mediated genre, but a hypertext essay on the character of Hamlet, with its links to scenes from the play and the commentary of Shakespeare scholars, will have more flash but not necessarily more substance than a print essay.

The widely held view that today's students are computer aficionados who enjoy working with computers is, literally, only half true. Surveying forty-two of her students from three sections of a first-year composition program that relies heavily on technology, Jones reports that 45 percent of her students rated technology as the least liked aspect of the course (289). Web page design is a component of Jones' program, and it was this exercise that drew the most negative response. Some students reported that computers made the writing process more difficult for them (289); two reported the course infected them with a "terrorizing phobia" (289) for computers. The "frequency with which a technological component was listed as a least liked aspect of the course and the deteriorated attitude toward computers reported by several students," Jones concludes, "are cause for concern, reflection, and more study" (289-91).

Computer champions argue that the computer enhances the content of student writing because, through the Internet, writers can quickly access reams of information they can incorporate into and thereby invigorate their writing assignments. But much of the information that comes from the Internet is not vetted so its authority and reliability may be questionable. Moreover, running along the edges of the Internet is a deep and wide sewer of child pornography and racist, sexist, and homophobic hate-speech sites, which taint to some extent all sources of Internet information. This is one reason why Internet citations in bibliographies at the end of articles in academic journals are still relatively rare. And the Internet has intensified the problem of plagiarism, since students can so easily download information, often in the form of finished essays, on virtually any assigned topic.

Internet research is further lauded because texts usually provide links to other related texts, which can be accessed with a click of a mouse. These texts, in turn, link to other related texts, allowing the researcher to narrow and refine his or her search for relevant and useful knowledge. The downside is that a researcher, a student, especially, can drift too far away from the original source and soon get lost in a labyrinth of hypertext information, struggling to separate the useful from the irrelevant, trying to determine which texts are authoritative and reliable and which are not. Charney suggests that current theory and research in rhetoric, cognitive psychology, and document design does not support hypertext research, that "hypertext may dramatically increase the burdens on both readers and writers" (241). The linked hypertexts of cyberspace might be a better metaphor for the human brain than the linear sentences and paragraphs of print, but the research in reading comprehension Charney cites suggests we process information more effectively one clear, unified, and coherent text at a time. The computer facilitates access to information but may inhibit the way we process information.

And the Winner Is . . .

By a narrow margin, the negative side carries the debate. True, students can submit near-letter-perfect copy now, with the help of spell and grammar checks and other software programs. True, their work in progress can be monitored and checked more than ever before by teachers and fellow students who can respond to a draft and make suggestions for revisions online. But letter-prefect copy can't conceal insipid content, nor can online review mediate the resentment that a face-to-face conference can, through body language and tone of voice. For a generation now, students have used computers to complete their writing assignments, yet there is little evidence to suggest that the overall quality of student writing is any better now than it was in the age of the typewriter. Concluding his literature review on computers and writing quality, a review that spans nearly twenty years of theory and research, Moran states that our hope that computers would improve student writing has been dashed. Computers may facilitate and accelerate, but they do not educate.

Chapter Seventeen
WRITING ACROSS THE CURRICULUM

As a writing teacher in an English department, you may be asked to participate in your college's Writing Across the Curriculum Program, perhaps as a member of the WAC committee, perhaps as a writing specialist who will assist a professor in another department who wants some help designing effective writing assignments and grading students' papers. You may even be asked to teach a special section of freshman composition for students pursuing a specific major. You might be asked to participate in, even design, a workshop on some aspect of composition pedagogy, to which faculty across campus will be invited. As a writing teacher, you need to have some background in the Writing Across the Curriculum movement.

What Is Writing Across the Curriculum?

Writing Across the Curriculum is an academic program that encourages all teachers to integrate writing assignments into their curricula. It is based upon the belief, articulated in the work of, among others, Janet Emig and Kenneth Bruffee, that writing is a powerful adjunct to learning and to learning assessment. Students master a subject and better retain what they learn when they write about that subject, because writing reifies learning, synthesizes knowledge, concretizes thought, impels critical thinking, and demands active engagement. Teachers, in turn, confirm that their students are learning by assessing their writing. Many colleges and universities employ a Writing Across the Curriculum director, whose job it is to increase the amount of writing done in university courses; to encourage all faculty to offer some instruction in effective writing, in the context of their own discipline; and to help all teachers become good writing teachers. The director is usually a faculty member in the English department or of a separate department or program responsible for improving learning and teaching across the college or university.

There are two schools of thought regarding the central focus of WAC programs. Some directors believe that teachers need to integrate more low-stakes writing assignments—journals and focused free-writes, for example—into their curricula to help students explore a subject independently and without pressure. Others believe the main purpose of the program is to help students write the high-stakes essays and reports, required in most disciplines, so they can get better grades. These directors sometimes reject the term "writing across the curriculum" and call their program, instead, Writing in the Disciplines. A third school of thought favors a reconciliation between the two positions and encourages program participants to help professors integrate all types of writing into their courses (McCleod 151).

Writing Across the Curriculum programs are entrenched now in many colleges and universities because there is substantial evidence that they have succeeded in their mission to help the college graduate highly literate students. Assessing the program at one university, Fulwiler admits there were challenges the program had to overcome but reports a general sense, university wide, that the program did help improve student writing. Ridley, Smith, and Mulligan assessed the writing skills of seventy-one college seniors and found that the best writers were those who had taken the most writing-intensive courses.

Genre Theory

Writing Across the Curriculum proponents find some justification for the program in genre theory. As a composition term, genre refers to a mode of written communication that shares linguistic and rhetorical characteristics, as dictated by social convention. The letter of application for employment, for example, is a genre of written discourse characterized by similar, socially sanctioned content and style. It will be formal, reserved, and polite; it will reveal personal information, especially that related to the writer's employment history. The writer brings to bear his or her knowledge of the conventions of the genre as he or she writes in it, and this knowledge will help his or her determine his or her purpose, generate content, and express himself or herself in appropriate language in an appropriate voice. The reader, too, will bring her knowledge of the genre of the letter of application to bear as she reads, and this knowledge will help her comprehend the letter and judge its merit.

One example of a rhetorical convention, the acceptability of which varies from one discipline to another, is the use of passive voice. The handbook you use in your English department writing program probably advises against it, because it is less direct and concise than active voice. "Our handbook recommends the use of active voice" is a clearer and more concise sentence than "The use of active voice is recommended by our handbook." Yet scientists, describing the results of their experiments, regularly use passive voice, writing, for example, "two milligrams of saline were added to the solution. . ." as opposed to "I added two milligrams of saline to the solution to. . . ." The first-person point of view is accepted, sometimes encouraged by humanities professors—"I liked this story because I could identify with the main character"—but frowned upon by scientists who prefer the more detached, impersonal tone the passive voice conveys. And, yes, I used passive voice in the preceding sentence. (In active voice, the sentence would read: "Humanities professors accept, sometimes encourage the first-person point of view. . . , but scientists frown upon it.") because I wanted the stress to be not on the professors but on the way in which voice affects point of view.

Document design also varies from one discipline to the next. Academic papers in the sciences and social sciences often include an abstract, are often divided into a series of headings and subheadings, and often include graphs, charts, and illustrations. Papers that report the results of a social science experiment, for example, usually begin with an abstract and are divided into such sections as Introduction, Method, Results, Discussion, and Conclusion. Convention dictates that these headings are centered on the page but not underlined. There may be subheadings, as well; for example, the Method section might be sub-divided into Subjects, Apparatus, Design, and Procedure. These subheadings are flush with the left margin and underlined or italicized. Humanities papers, on the other hand, tend to use fewer charts, graphs, and illustrations and a less formal system of headings, if they are used at all. Humanists take pride in their ability to transition from one idea to the next using rhetorical strategies as opposed to headings. And, of course, the format for citing sources, both within the essay, and in the source list also varies from one discipline to the next. Some disciplines use footnotes and endnotes, some cite sources in parenthesis within the essay, though the content of the parenthetical information also varies. There are also major differences in the format for the title, the placement of dates, the use of capital letters, and the use of quotation marks in the list of research sources at the end of the essay, depending upon the conventions of the discipline for which the paper was written.

The style in which academic papers are written also varies, depending upon the discipline within which the writer is working. Here is a brief passage from a journal for biology teachers:

For ecologists, the question of what happens to ecosystem functioning as biological diversity declines has substantial applied interest. Current extinction rates are orders of magnitude higher than throughout much of Earth's history (Lawton & May, 1995; Pimm et al., 1995). One consequence of this global loss of biodiversity may be impairment of the environmental goods and services on which humans depend (Costanza et al., 1997). Ecologists have addressed this issue directly by manipulating species number in small areas and recording properties such as standing biomass, soil nitrogen, or decomposition rates. Most of these studies have been carried out in terrestrial grasslands (Hector et al, 1999) or in microcosms using protist communities (Naeem & Li, 1997; McGrady-Steed et al., 1997). In many cases, strong positive relationships emerge between species richness and ecosystem functioning (Naeem et al., 1994, 1995; Tilman et al., 1996), but there are exceptions (Johnson et al., 1996). Other studies have demonstrated that more diverse communities are more stable in terms of resistance to disturbance, recovery after disturbance, or long-term invariability of production (Tilman & Downing, 1994; Naeem & Li, 1997; McGrady-Steed et al., 1997). (Ruesinck, O'Connor, and Sparks 285)

The paragraph has a clear and direct style. The sentences are comparatively brief and only two of the seven—the first and the last—are complex. The first and the sixth sentences open with a prepositional phrase, but the others begin with a subject. Biologists would be familiar with the specialized vocabulary—"protist communities," "standing biomass"—that would send the layman to the dictionary. Sources are cited carefully and include names and dates.

Here is a brief passage from a journal for English teachers:

So what should I do? The students had grabbed their hair and told me that learning punctuation was going to drive them crazy. Edgar H. Schuster agrees with their reaction—although he is referring to the editing rules used by publishing houses: "I don't mean to downplay these rules, since knowing them is empowering, but trying to teach and learn them has driven not a few teachers and students to the brink of substance abuse" (xii). The students need to pass the high-stakes ISAT made me disagree. Romano encourages students to break conventions—with a caveat. He advises, "I also want them to realize that if their writing is a mechanical disaster, their natural voice might be dismissed by others, regardless of how authentic, colorful, and pointed it is" (73). I believed that I had to protect students' ability to pass the ISAT and write successfully for grammatical purists. When students asked why they couldn't punctuate as some modern novelists did, I fell back on an explanation like the one Lynne Truss uses in his or her bestseller, *Eats, Shoots, and Leaves: The Zero Tolerance Approach to Punctuation.* She is referring to the comma splice, but I applied her words to all broken rules: "Done equally knowingly by people who are not published writers, it can look weak or presumptuous. Done ignorantly by ignorant people, it is awful" (88). (Warne 24)

How different is the tone, style, point of view, diction, and sentence structure of this paragraph compared to the one from the biology journal! The author's first sentence is a question, and, in her second, she describes students grabbing their hair, a deliberately amusing metaphor that would be out of place in a science journal. She uses first-person point of view, which the editors of science and social science journals will not usually accept. Her sentence structure is more varied and less formal than that used in the biology journal paragraph. Her diction is less discipline specific. She does not include dates in his or her citations; dates are required in citations in science and social science papers but usually not in humanities papers.

Writing Intensive Courses

Realizing that these discourse conventions are so different from one discipline to the next, administrators at many universities have designated certain courses in every department as "writing intensive" courses and have made it a policy for students to take a certain number of WI courses before they can graduate. That number varies from one college to the next, as does the definition of a writing-intensive course. In the interests of academic freedom, those definitions tend to be general rather than specific: "a substantial portion of the grade for this course will be based upon student writing," as opposed to "students must produce a minimum of 5,000 words of academic writing to complete the course successfully." Graduate students, in the role of teaching assistant, are often assigned to writing-intensive courses to help professors design and evaluate writing assignments.

If you have the opportunity to become a WAC teacher or TA (sometimes called a WIT, that is, a Writing Intensive Tutor), give the opportunity serious consideration. Graduate students in English may have a lock on first-year writing courses, but on occasion, educational administrators have been known to turn their distracted attention to the high cost of running first-year writing programs, and to wonder if both students and the institution would not be better served if the first-year writing program were abolished in favor of compulsory writing-intensive courses. And department chairs in disciplines other than English will sometimes recruit English graduate students to act as consultants for writing-intensive courses. You will increase your "marketability" if you make yourself an expert in the discourse conventions of a discipline other than your own.

To be sure, this is a challenge for English adjunct faculty and graduate students, but there are several excellent books that will help you rise to it. Barbara Walvoord's *Helping Students Write Well: A Guide for Teachers in All Disciplines* (2nd ed., 1986) provides an excellent introduction to writing in the disciplines, offering advice on how to design effective assignments and respond to student writing across the curriculum. Margot Soven's *Write to Learn: A Guide to Writing Across the Curriculum* (1996) offers advice on lower-stakes writing assignments, journals especially, that can be used effectively to help students master course content; she also offers advice about designing more formal academic assignments and includes an excellent array of models. Charles Bazerman and David Russell's *Landmark Essays on Writing Across the Curriculum* (1994) contains thirteen essays that will give you a sense of the history of writing across the curriculum and practical advice on assigning and grading essays from a variety of disciplines. Art Young's *Teaching Writing Across the Curriculum* (3rd ed. 1997) also validates the writing-learning connection with an array of pedagogical strategies useful to teachers who have been assigned to writing-intensive courses or teachers who want to integrate more writing into their curriculum. An excellent website is the WAC Clearinghouse at http://aw.colostate.edu/resource_list.htm.

Even with this knowledge, however, you will want some help and support from professors who are genuine specialists in the discipline for which you are providing some writing instruction. Be prepared for some resistance because professors in disciplines other than English often reject the call to provide some instruction in writing, even in the context of their own discipline, arguing that writing instruction is the province of the English department or the school of education. They will value good writing and understand the interdependence of writing and learning; they will want their students to be good writers; but they may feel unqualified to provide instruction. You might need to remind them, diplomatically, that every academic discourse has its own discourse conventions (see Blair) and that it is the conventions of the discourse of their discipline you need their help in providing. Writing is, in part, a social act, mediated by a social context controlled and sanctioned by members of the group, be they chemists, sociologists, economists, or lawyers. You, as an English language and literature specialist, can certainly teach all students how to research a topic, develop a plan, frame a thesis, write a draft, and revise and edit that draft. But you will need help from colleagues in other disciplines to understand the discourse conventions of that discipline. There is much truth to the WAC director's mantra: it takes a village to raise a writer.

WORKS CONSULTED

Anson, Chris, M. "Reflective Reading: Developing Thoughtful Ways to Respond to Student's Writing." *Evaluating Writing*. Eds. Charles R. Cooper and Lee Odell. Urbana, Illinois: National Council of Teachers of English, 1999. Rpt. in *The Allyn and Bacon Sourcebook for College Writing Teachers*. Ed. James C. McDonald. Boston: Allyn and Bacon, 2000. 374–393.

Bartholomae, David. "Inventing the University." *Cross Talk in Comp Theory*. Ed. Victor Villanueva Jr. Urbana, Illinois: NCTE, 1997. 589–619.

– – –. "The Study of Error." *College Composition and Communication* 31 (1980): 253–69.

Barton, Ellen L. "Interpreting the Discourses of Technology." Selfe and Hilligoss 56–75.

Bauer, Dale M. "The Other 'F' Word: The Feminist in the Classroom." *College English* 52 (1990): 385–96.

Beach, Richard. "Self-Evaluation Strategies of Extensive Revisers and Non-Revisers. *College Composition and Communication* 27 (May 1976): 160–64.

Beck, Charles R. "A Taxonomy for Identifying, Classifying, and Interrelating Teaching Strategies." *The Journal of General Education* 47 (1998): 37–62.

Becker, Angela H. and Sharon K. Calhoon. "What Introductory Psychology Students Attend to on a Course Syllabus." *Teaching of Psychology* 26 (1999): 6–12.

Berlin, James, A. "Rhetoric and Ideology in the Writing Class." *Cross Talk in Comp Theory: A Reader*. Ed. Victor Villanueva, Jr. Urbana, IL: National Council of Teachers of English, 1997. 679–700.

Blair, Catherine Pastore. "Only One of the Voices: Dialogic Writing Across the Curriculum." *College English* (50) April 1988): 383–89.

Bloom, Lynn Z. "The Essay Canon." *College English* 61 (March 1999): 401–430.

Braddock, Richard. "The Frequency and Placement of Topic Sentences in Expository Prose." *Research in the Teaching of English* 8.3 (Winter 1974): 287–302.

Braddock, Richard. "The Frequency and Placement of Topic Sentences in Expository Prose." *Research in the Teaching of English* 8 (1974): 287–302. Rpt. in *Cross Talk in Comp Theory: A Reader*. Ed. Victor Villanueva Jr. Urbana, Illinois: National Council of Teachers of English, 1997. 167–181.

Brody, Miriam. *Manly Writing: Gender, Rhetoric, and the Rise of Composition*. Carbondale and Edwardsville: Southern Illinois U. P., 1993.

Brooke, Robert, Ruth Mirtz, and Rick Evans. *Small Groups in Writing Workshops*. Urbana, Ill.: NCTE, 1994.

Brossell, Gordon. "Rhetorical Specification in Essay Examination Topics." *College English* 35 (1983): 165–173.

Burchfield, R.W. (Ed.). *The New Fowler's Modern English Usage*. 3rd ed. Oxford University Press, 1996.

Campbell, Linda, Bruce Campbell, and Dee Dickinson. *Teaching and Learning Through Multiple Intelligences*. 2nd ed. Needham Heights, MA: Allyn & Bacon, 1999.

Charney, Davida. "The Effect of Hypertext on Processes of Reading and Writing." Selfe and Hilligoss 238–63.

Charney, Davida H. and Richard A. Carlson. "Learning to Write in a Genre: What Student Writers Take from Model Texts." *Research in the Teaching of English* 29 (1995): 88–125.

Christensen, Francis. *Notes Toward a New Rhetoric: Six Essays for Teachers.* New York: Harper and Row, 1978.

Colavito, J. Rocky. "The Bytes Are On, But Nobody's Home: Composition's Wrong Turns in the Computer Age." *Reforming College Composition: Writing the Wrongs.* Eds. Ray Wallace, Alan Jackson, and Susan Lewis Wallace. Wesport, Connecticut: Greenwood Press, 2000. 149–59.

Coles, William E. Jr. *The Plural I: The Teaching of Writing.* New York: Holt, Rinehart and Winston, 1978. Portsmouth, NH: Boynton/Cook, 1988.

Corbett, Edward P.J. "Approaches to the Study of Style." *Teaching Composition: 10 Bibliographical Essays.* Ed. Gary Tate. Fort Worth: Texas Christian University Press, 1976. 63–109.

– – –. *Classical Rhetoric for the Modern Student.* 3rd ed. New York: Oxford University Press, 1990.

– – –. "Teaching Style." *Selected Essays of Edward P.J. Corbett.* Ed. Robert J. Connors. Southern Methodist University Press, 1989. Rpt. in *The Allyn & Bacon Sourcebook for College Writing Teachers.* 2nd ed. Ed. James C. McDonald. Needham Heights, MA: Allyn & Bacon, 2000. 295–305.

Costanzo, William. *Twelve Great Films on Video and How to Teach Them.* Urbana, IL: National Council of Teachers of English, 1992.

– – –. "Reading, Writing, and Thinking in an Age of Electronic Literacy." Selfe and Hilligoss 11–21.

Crowhurst, Marion. "Sentence Combining: Maintaining Realistic Expectations." *College Composition and Communication* 34 (1983): 62–71.

Daiker, Donald, Andrew Kerek, and Max Morenberg. "Sentence-Combining and Syntactic Maturity in Freshman English." *College Composition and Communication* 29 (1978): 36–41.

Daiute, Colette A. "Physical and Cognitive Factors in Revising: Insights from Studies with Computers." *Research in the Teaching of English* 20 (1986): 141–59.

Dale, Helen. *Co-Authoring the Classroom: Creating an Environment for Effective Collaboration.* Theory and Practice into Research Series. Urbana, IL: National Council of Teachers of English, 1997.

"Defining and Avoiding Plagiarism. The WPA Statement on Best Practices." January 2003. 29 November 2005 <http://www.wpacouncil.org>.

Devet, Bonnie. "Bringing Back More Figures of Speech into Composition." *Journal of Teaching Writing* 6 (1987): 293–304.

Diederich, Paul Bernard, John W. French, and Sibly T. Carlton. *Factors in Judgments of Writing Ability.* Research Bulletin RB–61. Princeton Educational Testing Service, 1961.

Dobrin, David. "Style Analyzers Once More." *Computers and Composition* 3.3 (1986): 22–32.

Duin, Ann Hill, and Craig Hansen. "Reading and Writing on Computer Networks as Social Construction and Social Interaction." Selfe and Hilligoss 89–112.

Dunn, Rita, Jeffrey S. Beaudry, and Angela Klavas. "Survey of Research on Learning Styles." *Educational Leadership* (1989): 50–58.

Dunn, Rita, and Kenneth Dunn. *Teaching Secondary Students Through Their Individual Learning Styles: Practical Approaches for Grades 7–13.* Boston: Allyn and Bacon, 1993.

Elbow. Peter. "Ranking, Evaluating, and Liking: Sorting Out Three Forms of Judgment." *The Allyn and Bacon Sourcebook for College Writing Teachers*. Ed. James C. McDonald. Boston: Allyn and Bacon, 2000. 394–411.

———. *Writing Without Teachers*. New York: OUP, 1973.

Emig, Janet. *The Composing Processes of Twelfth Graders*. Urbana, IL: NCTE, 1971.

———. "Writing as a Mode of Learning." *Cross Talk in Comp Theory: A Reader*. Ed. Victor Villanueva, Jr. Urbana, IL: National Council of Teachers of English, 1997. 7–15.

Faigley, Lester. "Names in Search of a Concept: Maturity, Fluency, Complexity, and Growth in Written Syntax." *College Composition and Communication* 31 (1980): 291–300.

Feeser, Bonnie. "The Genius Sitting Next to Me: Celebrating Multiple Intelligences in the College Composition Classroom." Thesis. Wichita State University, 2002.

Flannery, Kathryn. *The Emperor's New Clothes: Literature, Literacy, and the Ideology of Style*. Pittsburgh: University of Pittsburgh Press, 1995.

Flower, Linda S., John R. Hayes, Linda Carey, Karen Schriver, and James Stratman. "Detection, Diagnosis, and the Strategies of Revision. *College Composition and Communication* 37 (February 1986): 16–55.

Flynn, Elizabeth A. "Composing as a Woman." *College Composition and Communication* 39 (1988): 423–35.

Forman, Janis. "Literacy, Technology, and Collaboration: New Connections and Challenges." Selfe and Hilligoss 130–43.

Foster, David. *A Primer for Writing Teachers: Theories, Theorists, Issues, Problems*. 2nd ed. Portsmouth, NH: Boynton/Cook Heinemann, 1992.

———. "Reading(s) in the Writing Classroom." *College Composition and Communication* 48 (1997): 518–539.

Foster, Donald. *Author Unknown: Tales of a Literary Detective*. New York: Henry Holt, 2000.

Freedman, Sarah. *Response to Student Writing*. Urbana, Illinois: National Council of Teachers of English, 1987.

Freeman, Kimberly. "Your Life Is a C+: Assigning and Assessing the Personal Essay in First-Year Composition." Conference on College Composition and Communication. Phoenix, AZ 13 March 1997.

Fulkerson, Richard. "Composition at the Turn of the Twenty-First Century." *Collge Composition and Communication* 56 (June 2005): 654–687.

———. "Composition Theory in the Eighties: Axiological Consensus and Paradigmatic Diversity." *College Composition and Communication* 41 (1990): 409–29.

Fulwiler, Toby and Alan Hayakawa. *The Blair Handbook*. 4th ed. Upper Saddle River, NJ: Prentice Hall, 2003.

———. "How Well Does Writing Across the Curriculum Work?" *College English* 46 (February 1984): 113–25

George, Diana. "Working with Peer Groups in the Composition Classroom." *College Composition and Communication* 35 (October 1984): 320–326.

Gere, Anne Ruggles. "Teaching Writing: The Major Theories." *The Allyn and Bacon Sourcebook for College Writing Teachers*. Ed. James C. McDonald. Needham Heights, MA: Allyn and Bacon, 2000.

Gibson, Walker. *Tough, Sweet, and Stuffy: An Essay on Modern American Prose Style*. Bloomington: Indiana UP, 1966.

Glenn, Cheryl, Melissa A. Goldthwaite, and Robert Connors. *The St. Martin's Guide to Teaching Writing.* 5th ed. Boston: Bedford/St. Martins, 2003.

Gregorc, Anthony. *An Adult's Guide to Style.* Maynard, MA: Gabriel Systems, 1982.

Grimm, Nancy. "Improving Students' Responses to Their Peers' Essays." *College Composition and Communication* 38 (1986): 91–94.

Hacker, Diana. *The Blair Handbook.* 6th ed. Boston: Bedford/St. Martins, 2002.

Hacker, Tim. "The Effect of Teacher Conferences on Peer Response Discourse." *Teaching English in the Two-Year College* 27 (May 1996): 112–126.

Hardy-Lucas, Faye. "Constructing Legally Sound Syllabi." 2004. Hampton University Center for Teaching Excellence. 18 November 2005 <http://www.hamptonu.edu/administration/provost/cte/whitepapers/legally_sound.htm>.

Harrison, Deanna. "Accommodating All Learning Styles in the College Composition Classroom." Thesis. Wichita State University, 2002.

Hartwell, Patrick. "Grammar, Grammars, and the Teaching of Grammar." *College English* 47 (1985): 105–27.

Hawisher, Gail, and Cynthia Selfe. "The Rhetoric of Technology and the Electronic Writing Class." *College Composition and Communication* 42 (1991): 55–65.

Heller, Mary F. "The Reading-Writing Connection: An Analysis of the Written Language of University Freshmen at Two Reading Levels." 1980. ERIC ED 216 342.

Hennessy, Michael. "Readers in the Composition Course: Why They Fail, How We Can Make Them Work." March 1982. ERIC ED 214 187.

Hillocks, George, Jr. *Research in Written Composition: New Directions for Teaching.* Urbana, IL: National Council of Teachers of English, 1986.

Holdstein, Deborah, H. "Gender, Feminism, and Institution-Wide Assessment Programs." *Assessment of Writing: Politics, Policies, Practices.* Ed. Edward M. White, William D. Lutz, and Sandra Kamusikiri. New York: The Modern Language Association of America, 1996. 204–225.

Horvath, Brooke K. "The Components of Written Response: A Practical Synthesis of Current Views." *Rhetoric Review* 2(1984): 136–56. Rpt. in *The Writing Teacher's Sourcebook*, 4th ed. Eds. Edward P. J. Corbett, Nancy Myers, and Gary Tate. New York: Oxford University Press, 2000. 243–257.

Howard, Rebecca Moore. "Collaborative Pedagogy." *A Guide to Composition Pedagogies.* Eds. Gary Tate, Amy Rupiper, and Kurt Schick. New York: Oxford UP, 2001.

Hunt, Kellogg. *Grammatical Structures Written at Three Grade Levels.* NCTE Research Report # 3. Urbana, IL: NCTE, 1965.

Jones, Billie J. "Learning with, through, and about Computers: Students' Best Friend or Worst Nightmare?" *Teaching English in the Two-Year College* 30 (2003): 286–95.

Julier, Laura. "Community Service Pedagogy." *A Guide to Composition Pedagogies.* Eds. Gary Tate, Amy Rupiper, and Kurt Schick. New York: Oxford UP, 2001.

Kent, Thomas. Ed. *Post-Process Theory: Beyond the Writing Process Paradigm.* Carbondale: Southern Illinois UP, 1999.

Kiefer, Kathleen E., and Charles Moran. "Textual Analysis with Computers: Tests of Bell Laboratories' Computer Software." *Research in the Teaching of English* 17 (1983): 201–14.

Kolln, Martha. "Everyone's Right to Their Own Language." *College Composition and Communication* 37 (1986): 100–102.

Lamb, Catherine E. "Beyond Argument in Feminist Composition." *College Composition and Communication* 42 (1991): 11–24.

Lamm, Robert Lawrence. "Primary Trait Scales, Revision, and Models: The Effects of Eight-Week Foci on Instruction on the Quality of Argumentative Essays Written by First-Year College Composition Students." Diss. University of Oklahoma, 1994.

Lanham, Richard, A. *Analyzing Prose*. New York: Charles Scribner's Sons, 1983.

———. *Revising Prose*, 3rd. ed. New York: Prentice Hall, 1991.

LeBlanc, Paul. "The Politics of Literacy and Technology in Secondary School Classrooms." Selfe and Hilligoss 22–36.

Lindemann, Erika. *A Rhetoric for Writing Teachers*. 4th ed. New York: Oxford UP, 2001.

Loban, Walter. *Language Development: Kindergarten Through Grade Twelve*. Urbana, IL: NCTE, 1976.

Lunsford, Andrea, and Lisa Ede. *Singular Texts/Plural Authors: Perspectives on Collaborative Writing*. Carbondale: Southern Illinois Univ. Press, 1990.

McCarthy, Bernice. "A Tale of Four Learners: 4MATs Learning Styles." *Educational Leadership* 54.6 (1997): 46–51.

McLeod, Susan. "The Pedagogy of Writing Across the Curriculum." *A Guide to Composition Pedagogies*. Ed. Gary Tate, Amy Rupiper, and Kurt Schick. New York: Oxford University Press, 2001. 149–164.

Manzo, Kathleen Kennedy. "NAEP Results Underscore Need to Up Writing Instruction." *Education Week*. (August 6, 2003): 10–11.

Marsh, Bill. "Turnitin.com and the Scriptural Enterprise of Plagiarism Detection." *Computers and Composition* 21.4 (2004): 427–38.

Miles, Libby. "Constructing Composition: Reproduction and WPA Agency in Textbook Publishing." *Writing Program Administrator* 24 (Fall/Winter 2000): 27–51.

Milic, Louis T. "Theories of Style and Their Implications for Teaching Composition." *College Composition and Communication* 16 (1965): 66–69, 126.

Moran, Charles. "Computers and Composition 1983–2002: What We Have Hoped For." *Computers and Composition* 20.4 (2003): 343–58.

Moran, Mary Hurley. "Connections between Reading and Successful Revision." *Journal of Basic Writing* 16 (Fall 1997): 76–89.

Morgan, Dan. "Ethical Issues Raised by Students' Personal Writing." *College English* 60 (1998): 318–325.

Murray, Donald. "Internal Revision: A Process of Discovery." *Research on Composing: Points of Departure*. Eds. Charles R. Cooper and Lee Odell. Urbana, IL: National Council of Teachers of English, 1978. 85–105.

———. "Writing as Process: How Writing Finds Its Own Meaning." *Eight Approaches to Teaching Composition*. Ed. Timothy R. Donovan and Ben W. McClelland. Urbana, IL: National Council of Teachers of English.

Myers-Breslin, Linda. "Technology, Distance, and Collaboration: Where Are These Pedagogies Taking Composition?" *Reforming College Composition: Writing the Wrongs*. Eds. Ray Wallace, Alan Jackson, Susan Lewis Wallace. Wesport, Connecticut: Greenwood Press, 2000. 161–77.

Myers, Isabel Briggs with Peter B. Myers. *Gifts Differing: Understanding Personality Type*. Palo Alto: Davies-Black, 1980.

Newkirk, Thomas. "Direction and Misdirection in Peer Response." *College Composition and Communication* 35 (1984):301–311.

Noguchi, Rei R. *Grammar and the Teaching of Writing: Limits and Possibilities*. Urbana: National Council of Teachers of English, 1991.

Odell, Lee. "Writing Assessment and Learning to Write: A Classroom Perspective." *Theory and Practice in the Teaching of Writing: Re-thinking the Discipline*. Ed. Lee Odell. Carbondale: Southern Illinois University Press. 289–313.

O'Hare, Frank. *Sentence Combining: Improving Student Writing Without Formal Grammar Instruction*. NCTE Research Report #15. Urbana, IL: NCTE, 1973.

Palmquist, Mike. "A Brief History of Computer Support for Writing Centers and Writing-Across-the-Curriculum Programs." *Computers and Composition* 20.4 (2003): 395–413.

Perl, Sondra. "The Composing Process of Unskilled College Writers." *Cross Talk in Comp Theory: A Reader*. Ed Victor Villanueva Jr. Urbana, IL: National Council of Teachers of English, 1997. 17–39.

Peterson, Linda. "Repetition and Metaphor in Composing." *College Composition and Communication* 36 (1985): 429–43.

Peterson, Patricia Webb. "The Debate about Online Learning: Key Issues for Writing Teachers." *Computers and Composition* 18.4 (2001): 359–70.

Podis, Leonard, A. and Joanne M. Podis. "Improving Our Responses to Student Writing: A Process-Oriented Approach." *Rhetoric Review* 5.1 (1986): 90–98. Rpt. in *The Allyn and Bacon Sourcebook for College Writing Teachers*. Ed. James C. McDonald. Boston: Allyn and Bacon, 2000. 366–373.

Price, Margaret. "Beyond 'Gotcha!': Situating Plagiarism in Policy and Pedagogy." *College Composition and Communication* 54 (September 2002): 88–115

Raimes, Ann. *Universal Keys for Writers*. Boston: Houghton Mifflin, 2004.

Ridley, Dennis R., Edward D. Smith, and Roark Mulligan. "Writing Across the Curriculum Works: The Impact of Writing Emphasis upon Senior Exit Writing Samples." A paper presented at the ASHE Annual Meeting, November 2000.

Rimer, Sara. "A Campus Fad That's Being Copied: Internet Plagiarism Seems on the Rise." *New York Times* 3 September 3: B7.

Ronald, Kate. "Style: The Hidden Agenda in Composition Classes." *The Subject is Writing: Essays by Teachers and Students*. 3rd. ed. Ed. Wendy Bishop. Portsmouth, NH: Heinemann Boynton/Cook, 2003. 195–209.

Ruesink, Jennifer, Eileen O'Connor, and Grace Sparks. "Biodiversity & Ecosystem Functioning: Exploring Principles of Ecology with Agricultural Plants." *The American Biology Teacher* 68 (May 2006): 285–293.

Salvatorie, Mariolina. "Conversations with Texts: Reading in the Teaching of Composition." *College English* 58 (1996): 440–455.

Scharton, Maurice. "The Politics of Validity." *Assessment of Writing: Politics, Policies, Practices*. Ed. Edward M. White, William D. Lutz, and Sandra Kamusikiri. New York: The Modern Language Association of America, 1996. 53–75.

Selfe, Cynthia L., and Susan Hilligoss, eds. *Literacy and Computers: The Complications of Teaching and Learning with Technology*. New York: Modern Language Association, 1994.

Shepherd-Wynn, Evelyn G. *The Effect of Collaborative Learning on English Composition Students' Writing Anxiety, Apprehension, Attitude and Writing Quality.* Diss. Grambling State U., 1999.

Smagorinsky, Peter. "How Reading Model Essays Affects Writers." *Reading/Writing Connections: Learning from Research.* Ed. Judith W. Irwin. Newark: International Reading Association, 1992. 174–190.

Soles, Derek. "Practical Instruction in Editing Conventions." *The Oregon English Journal* XXIII.1 (2001): 15–18.

———. "Teaching Pronoun-Antecedent Agreement with Gender-Neutral Nouns." *Kentucky English Bulletin* 47.2 (1998): 29–34.

Sommers, Nancy. "Responding to Student Writing." *College Composition and Communication* 33 (1982): 148–56. Rpt. in *The New St. Martin's Guide to Teaching Writing.* Robert Connors and Cheryl Glenn. Boston: Bedford/St. Martins, 1999. 339–347.

———. "Revision Strategies of Student Writers and Experienced Adult Writers." *College Composition and Communication* 31 (December 1980): 378–88.

Sommers, Nancy. "Revision Strategies of Student Writers and Experienced Adult Writers." *College Composition and Communication* 31 (December 1980): 378–88.

Spears, Karen. *Sharing Writing.* Portsmouth, NH: Boynton Cook, 1988.

Spear, Karen. *Sharing Writing: Peer Response Groups in English Classes.* Portsmouth, N.H.: Heinemann-Boynton/Cook, 1988.

Stoddard, Barbra and Charles A. MacArthur. "A Peer Editor Strategy: Guiding Learning-Disabled Students in Response and Revision." *Research in the Teaching of English* 27 (1993): 76–103.

Stolarek, Elizabeth A. "Prose Modeling and Metacognition: The Effect of Modeling on Developing a Metacognitive Stance toward Writing." *Research in the Teaching of English* 28 (1994): 154–174.

Straub, Richard and Ronald F. Lunsford. *Twelve Readers Reading: Responding to College Student Writing.* Cresskill, N.J.: Hampton Press, 1995.

Strunk, William, Jr., E.B. White, and Roger Angell. *The Elements of Style.* 4th ed. Needham Heights: Allyn and Bacon, 2000.

Sudol, Ronald A. "Applied Word Processing: Notes on Authority, Responsibility, and Revision in a Workshop Model." *College Composition and Communication* 36 (1985): 331–35.

———. (Ed). *Revising: New Essays for Teachers of Writing.* Urbana, IL: National Council of Teachers of English, 1982.

Tarvers, Josephine. "The Composing Process: An Overview." *Simon and Schuster Handbook for Writers.* 3rd ed., Annotated Instructor's Edition by Lynn Quitman Troyka. Englewood Cliffs, New Jersey: Prentice Hall, 1993.

Taylor, Harold. "Listening Comprehension and Reading Comprehension as Predictors of Achievement in College Composition." Diss. University of Washington. DAI 42 (1981): 66-A.

"Teaching About Plagiarism in a Digital Age." *The Council Chronicle* November 2005: 1, 8–9.

Tierney, R.J. and P.D. Pearson. "Toward a Composing Model of Reading." *Language Arts* 60 (1983): 568–580.

Timbur, John. "Consensus and Difference in Collaborative Learning." *College English* 51 (1989): 602–16.

Tobin, Lad. "Process Pedagogy." In Gary Tate, Amy Rupiper, and Kurt Schick Eds. *Guide to Composition Pedagogies*. New York: Oxford UP, 2001.

Toosi, Nahal. "Internet Gives Rise to a Bold New Era in College-Student Cheating." *Milwaukee Journal Sentinel* 19 January 2004. 21 November 2005 <http://web.lexis-nexis.com>.

Tuzi, Frank. "The Impact of e-feedback on the revisions of L2 Writers in an Academic Writing Course." *Computers and Composition* 21.2 (2004): 217–35.

Valeri-Gold, Maria, and Mary P. Deming. "Reading, Writing, and the College Developmental Student." *Handbook of College Reading and Study Strategy Research*. Eds. Rona F. Flippo and David C. Caverly. Mahwah, NJ: Lawrence Erlbaum, 2000. 149–173.

Wahlstrom, Billie J. "Communication and Technology: Defining a Feminist Presence in Research and Practice." Selfe and Hilligoss 171–85.

Walpole, Jane. "The Vigorous Pursuit of Grace and Style." *Writing Instructor* 1 (1982): 163–69.

Warne, Bonnie Mary. "Teaching Conventions in a State-Mandated Testing Context." *English Journal* 95.5 (May 2006): 22–27.

Weathers, Winston. "Teaching Style: A Possible Anatomy." *College Composition and Communication* 21 (1970): 144–49. Rpt. in *The Writing Teachers' Sourcebook*. 4th ed. Eds. Edward P.J. Corbett, Nancy Myers, Gary Tate. New York: Oxford University Press, 2000. 368–373.

Weaver, Constance. *Teaching Grammar in Context*. Portsmouth, NH: Boynton/Cook, 1996.

White, Edward M. *Assigning, Responding, Evaluating: A Writing Teacher's Guide*. Boston/New York: Bedford/St. Martins, 1999.

———. "Power and Agenda Setting in Writing Assessment." *Assessment of Writing: Politics, Policies, Practices*. Ed. Edward M. White, William D. Lutz, and Sandra Kamusikiri. New York: The Modern Language Association of America, 1996. 9–24.

———. "The Scoring of Writing Portfolios: Phase 2." *College Composition and Communication* 56 (2005): 581–600.

———. *Teaching and Assessing Writing*. 2nd ed. San Francisco: Jossey-Bass, 1994.

Williams, James D. *Preparing to Teach Writing: Research, Theory, and Practice*. 3rd. edition. Mahwah, NJ: Lawrence Erlbaum Associates, 2003.

Williams, Joseph M. "The Phenomenology of Error." *College Composition and Communication* 32 (1981): 152–168.

———. *Style: Ten Lessons in Clarity and Grace*. 7th ed. Boston: Longman, 2002.

Witte, Stephen P., and Lester Faigley. "Coherence, Cohesion, and Writing Quality." *College Composition and Communication* 32 (1981): 189–204.

Wolcott, Willa with Sue M. Legg. *An Overview of Writing Assessment: Theory, Research, and Practice*. Urbana, Illinois: National Council of Teachers of English, 1998.

"WPA Outcomes Statement for First-Year Composition." *WPA: Writing Program Administration* 23.1/2 (Fall/Winter 1999): 59–66.

Wresch, William. "The Challenges of Creating Networked Connections among Teachers and Students." Selfe and Hilligoss 186–91.

Wyngaard, Sandra and Rachel Gehrke, "Responding to Audience: Using Rubrics to Teach and Assess Writing." *English Journal* 85.6 (1996): 67–70.

Yagaelski, Robert. "The Role of Classroom Context in the Revision Strategies of Student Writers." *Research in the Teaching of English* 29 (May 1995): 216–238.

Young, Richard E. "Paradigms and Problems: Needed Research in Rhetorical Invention." *Research on Composing: Points of Departure*. Eds. Charles R. Cooper and Lee Odell. Urbana, IL: National Council of Teachers of English, 1978. 29–47.

Zeni, Jane. "Literacy, Technology, and Teacher Education." Selfe and Hilligoss 76–86.

Zhu, Wei. "Effects of Training for Peer Response on Students' Comments and Interaction." *Written Communication* 12 (October 1995): 492–528.

INDEX